Hockey Talk

The game's language that you'll <u>never</u> pick up
from watching television!

ROBERT DAVIES

Canadian Cataloguing in Publication Data

Poteet, Lewis J.
  Hockey Talk
  Includes bibliographical references and index.
  Previously published as : The hockey phrase book. Mont
  real : Occasion Books, 1987.

ISBN 1-895854-56-3

  1. Hockey - Dictionaries. 2. Hockey - Anecdotes.   I.
Poteet, Aaron C.   II. Title.   III. Title: Hockey Phrase book.

GV847.P68 1996   796.962'03   C96-940367-4

If you would like to receive our catalog of publications, please write to:
Robert Davies Publishing
P.O. Box 702, Outremont, Quebec, Canada H2V 4N6
or e-mail a request to rdppub@vir.com

Lewis J. Poteet
and Aaron Poteet

Hockey Talk

Robert Davies Publishing
MONTREAL-TORONTO-PARIS

This book may be ordered in Canada from
General Distribution Services
☎1-800-387-0141 / 1-800-387- 0172 FAX 1-416-445-5967;

in the U.S.A., from
General Distribution Services,
Suite 202, 85 River Rock Drive, Buffalo, NY 14287
☎ 1-800-805-1083

or call the publisher, toll-free throughout North America:
1-800-481-2440, FAX 1-888-RDAVIES

e-mail: rdppub@vir.com

Visit our Internet website:
http://rdppub.com

The publisher takes this opportunity to thank the
Canada Council and the Ministère de la Culture
du Québec for their continuing support of publishing.

CONTENTS

PREFACE

Like many sports, hockey is both old and new. As a form of stickball, it is centuries old, but its special language, in English, has not been seriously studied until now.

It has become a major centre of interest and activity for many people, mainly male, in areas of the North American and European continents not ice-deprived. *One Sports Illustrated* survey has placed its popularity in the United States at 12th among sports, behind rodeo and wrestling, but it surely has a higher standing in such northern cities as Boston, New York, Chicago, Madison and Minneapolis. In Canada, certainly, it is a focus for intense play for many men and boys, and now some women and girls, from fall to spring, not just as spectators of the big-money professional games but also as activity and topic for discussion. Hockey is, among other things, a very large speech community. To get ourselves ready to speak for this community, we have gathered phrases from many sources, centering on Montreal, surely the hockey capital of the world. Most of these phrases have come up in play.

One of the reasons why hockey is so vital and energetic, why it is a world of its own, is that its heart is the informal street or outdoor rink pickup game. Played with ball or puck, on ice or pavement, wearing skates, tennis shoes, or moccasins, these games – in spaces sometimes overcrowded and with the most informal of agreed-upon rules – bring together people of all ages and ranges of experience and skill. Players take longer shifts than the thirty-seconds to two minutes customary in more organized games; they learn better stickhandling because they have to compete; the ice is rougher than at the Forum or Boston Gardens, so balance is tested and they use the snow to start and stop. And every game is good for talk, before, during, and after.

The intense attention paid star hockey players means they have an influence on the speech of the whole community, but they by no means determine its limits. Regional differences are real and enduring. We have worked particularly on differences between New England and Quebec. In Quebec, both English and French folk vocabularies are in use, but they are used together, with words and phrases interchangeable for greater clarity or word-play.

Hockey talk has shared many terms with other sports. Basketball, a sister (or brother) sport of about the same age, shares most with it, but terms are adapted or loaned to baseball, football, soccer, and so forth. We have tried to note these common terms.

W.P. Kinsella has said that baseball players' nicknames have become less colorful over the years (CBC Morningside, November 5, 1983). We have included many nicknames of hockey players to provide a basis for comparison. It is common in pickup games for players to know only each other's first names, or nicknames (for a special instance, see No-Name League). But the vigor of nicknaming is only one aspect of the evolution of hockey talk. Many students of the game have said that hockey language has gotten more technical and less colorful over the years. It is possible that the movement called "scientific," with its emphasis on kinetics, precision of terminology, and carefully diagrammed plays, has influenced such a tendency. The expansion of the original National Hockey League and the enormous growth of the hockey public through televising of games have certainly meant that hockey had to be made intelligible to many new fans, and simplicity and clarity are necessary to the spread of language in the urban setting.

But hockey talk would not have its character, and hockey would not have its strength as an absorbing world of its own, if these changes had been complete, or even major in impact. Studies have been made on the reinforcing effect of verbal interaction on team sports. Or to say it another way, when players meet in a Boston rink with no dressing rooms, only a curtain across one corner behind which both teams must dress, there is less talk in the "dressing room" than when they have proper rooms, with teammates only. On the ice, when this has happened, there is more talk.

HOCKEY TALK

At a time in the history of the sport when many are saying that the era of great hockey is over (A perennial prediction: it happened when goalie masks were introduced, when helmets became customary, when slapshots were invented, when expansion multiplied franchises and leagues), we think it important not to lose perspective. The current crisis seems to come from the fear that violence and drug use have gotten out of control, have "taken over the game." A major article on this subject in *Sports Illustrated* in 1986 drew a lot of attention to this question. But we may keep perspective by looking beyond the moment and the media to the enduring body of words in this subgroup culture of work and play. The words contain it all, and reflect it accurately and colorfully. The violence, the skill, the cruelty, the anger, the mutual helpfulness – all are there. And as long as the interest in a vital human activity endures, so will the language go on being a mirror world to the world of the sport. Play in one produces and reflects play in the other.

Ice Hockey Then and Now

by *Alyce Taylor Cheska*
University of Illinois
Urbana-Champaign, Illinois, U.S.A.

Did you ever swing at an object with a stick – probably so, because striking at something seems to be a universal activity. Add a smooth surface, a goal to each end, some one to play against, and the basic ingredients of a hockey game are present. When some pre determined scoring criterion is reached, a winner is declared.

Games have been recorded since antiquity. Authoiities have traced the stick and stone game back to 2000 B.C. in Persia and to 500 B.C. in Greece (Considine, 1982). These ancient ball games were usually played on certain festival or fete days, honoring early pagan gods of agriculture and fertility. Herodotus, the Greek chronicler, when travelling in Northern Africa in 450 B.C., observed a stick and stone combat which could be called a ritual hockey match (Henderson, 1947). The match was between two groups, one representing winter and the other summer. This "hockey" match was much more violent than hockey games today because the opponents literally killed each other. Some 700 years later St. Augustine tried to dissuade similar furious combats, but with little success; such stick and stone combats were observed in Algiers as late as 1921. In Algeria a game called "Koora" (ball), closely resembling hockey, was played at least into the 1930s. Since it was played only during the Christmas season, the connection with the religious life of the people is indicated (Gini, 1939; Simri, Uriel 1968). Westermarck (1926) recorded in one tribal group a kind of hockey ritual game played by women who used large ladles, while in another tribal group sticks were used. When the men and youth of the Libyan villages played a ball with sticks, it was considered a ritual to produce rain (Westermarck, 1926).

Henderson (1947) who has traced the origin of the stick ball game back to the Persians found that two variations were used. One version was based on striking the ball with a club, either on foot or on horseback (polo). The flattened club head provided a hard rebounding surface that lent itself to passing the ball along the ground. Over the years in order to better anticipate the direction and action of the ball, the area of play was gradually made smoother, more even, and finally low walls were constructed around the playing grounds. (A low walled court used for polo in 800 A.D. has been excavated in Asia Minor). These games were brought to Spain and southern France with the conquering Moors, and became deeply entrenched in the lives of the people. In spite of the opposition of the Christian Church to these vigorous ball folk-customs, they were hard to eradicate. Henderson reports,

> Perhaps the earliest form of the pagan rite, after it had become Christianized in Europe was the traditional game of 'la soule' as found in France in the twelfth century. It approximated very closely the old Moorish customs: there was the same taking of sides between large groups, sometimes divided regionally and sometimes by marital conditions. There was the same centering about the ball; the same use of sticks, large, small, curved, or stringed. There was the same association of the game with the springtime of the year, now called Easter or Shrovetide. (Henderson 1947, p. 39)

The stick ball game called "La soule" was played by the nobility, the ecclesiastics, and even by kings as well as by commoners. Frequent parish tournaments put all the countryside in a festive mood. In La soule, the ball was advanced in several ways, depending upon which version was being played; the ball, usually made of wood or of leather stuffed with bran, hemp, wool, could be driven with the foot, the hand, or varying shaped sticks (Henderson, 1947, p. 40). Ancient stick and ball game versions differ from hockey of today because of the large numbers of players involved; up to a thousand players were known to participate on each side. Since the whole community took part in the ritual celebration of which the game was part, all men were also expected to participate in the ritual game. In the evening after the game there was drinking and dancing and general merrymaking, for the players comprised all the village. The women were the spectators, pre and post game dancers, and food preparers. One wonders how much sexual roles have changed since those days?

In the 1300s A.D. one term "ad soulem crossare" suggested a stick for advancing the ball. Medieval writings describe a version of the above game as "chicane," which was played with clubs by a large number of players on each side. Each team tried to advance the ball with their clubs toward a goal line or upright post. The name "goal," meaning "score," grew from the Medieval European practice of trying to move the ball through the "goal" (gate) of one's opponents or one's own walled town, thus winning the game. The game of La Soule was carried from Brittany to Britain, from which local ball customs resembling a game of hockey developed, such as hurling in Cornwall and Ireland and shinty in Scotland. The older forms of play were traditional club-and-ball games, usually held in the spring of the year (Henderson, 1947, pp. 85-86). Goff, or Bandy-Ball, an ancestor of modern hockey, was a simple game played with small, hard, leather balls stuffed with feathers and a curved club, the end of which was covered with a piece of horn or metal. The object was to drive the ball between two small sticks set up in the ground or from one post to another some distance away (Moss, 1962, p. 59). In Britain, hockey is recognized as the descendant of hurling, shinty, and bandy. Moss describes the change,

From a rough game of 1850 with its twenty-a-side teams, its unlimited pitch, its shoulder chargings and legalized hammering of shins with the stick to get possession of the hard rubber ball, Hockey gradually mellowed through the thirty years. Rules were gradually added, overhauled, and amended so that by the end of the century, instead of the murderous brawl it had been fifty years earlier, Hockey was considered fit even for young ladies to play. (1962, p. 154).

A variety of hurling in Ireland consisted of hurling or throwing a heavy ball to a given point in the fewest number of throws. The total throws did not count, but only the net difference between the contestants as the game proceeded. It is possible that this form of the game could have influenced the development of golf. Also a secondary form of the game of shinty has been considered a possible source of golf. The game consisted of opposing sides who drove the ball with a stick or "caman" (Scottish word for club) into a series of holes (Henderson, 1947, pp. 89-90).

In Holland the concept of golf or Kolven, another stick/ball game, involved hitting a ball with a club from a distant spot into a hole or against a stick with as few swings as possible. Similar to hurling, the number of strokes between paired opponents was compared to determine the winner. Depending upon the season, a player "teed" up the ball on a piece of raised turf or snow. This popular game was played in winter months on the frozen canals of Holland. (See paintings of Peter Breughel the Elder's "January: the Return of the Hunters" (1565) and Hendrick Avercamp's "The Scene on the Ice Near a Town" (1625).

Paralleling through history the club-like stick games are those based on catching, throwing, or carrying a ball with a netted racket (a stick with woven webbing attached onto the curved end). With a netted racket the ball was advanced primarily through aerial passes and running with the ball nestled in the loose bag-like pocket of the racket. The North American Iroquois lacrosse racket is an example. One intriguing evidence regarding the history of Lacrosse in North America is that the French explorers, fishermen, and traders observed the Indians playing a stick ball game "battagaway" with a curved netted stick which in many respects resembled the French popular game "jeu de lacrosse," played with a curved stick (Charlevois, 1761). The Indians maneuvred a netted stick to catch, carry, and throw the ball. The rackets of several Indian tribes in southeastern United

States such as Cherokee, Choctaw, Chickasaw, however, had the string stretched taut, so the game was based on rebounding strategies. Two rackets were used instead of one of the northern *groups.*

Some authors suggest the game of shinny as progenitor to hockey, and that the North American Indians may have been introduced to and played shinny-style hockey concurrent with or earlier than the Europeans, both receiving the game indirectly from the ancient Egyptian fertility rites. In the 1500s and 1600s with the colonization by the Spanish and Portuguese in South America, the Indians of Chile were observed playing a game of shinny. The stick was flattened on the front face of the stick's bottom curve, much like the modern ice hockey stick. A sketch of such a game, La Sueca, appeared in 1712 (Henderson, 1947, p. 189). The Swedish anthropologist Nordenskiold (1910) reported such a shinny game played by the Araucanian Indians of Chile. It is well documented that ball games were very popular among the native American Indians. Throughout North America from the Arctic to the Caribbean many versions of the game of shinny have been recorded (Cheska, 1981; Culin, 1907; Smith, 1972). Nelson (1899) reported a game he called hockey "al'-yu-tal'-u-g'it" or "pat-k'u-tal-u-g'it" played by Alaskan Inuit (Eskimos). Nelson wrote: This is played with a small ball of ivory, leather, or wood, and a stick curved at the lower end. The ball and stick are called pat-k'u'tuk. The ball is placed on the ground or ice and the players divide into two parties. Each player with his stick attempts to drive the ball across the opponents'goal, which is established as in the football game. (1899, p. 337).

The central and eastern coastal Inuit (Eskimo) peoples probably played hockey-like games; but an exact description has not been recorded. In reports of the Danish Archeological Expeditions among the Arctic peoples in the first quarter of this century is mentioned a game of "keep away" played on ice. Each team tried to pass a stuffed leather ball between its own members, while the opposing team attempted to intercept the ball and then pass it to its own members (Rusmussen, 1930). Another game was "whip top," in which a ball was struck by a multi-stranded whip around the perimeter of the snow houses. The two teams each attempted to intercept the other's "top" or ball and reverse directions. No mention is made of using sticks, but the use of long bones for striking balls has been reported. A ball game, "aqsaqtuk," similar to football or Rugby, was played both in Alaska and on the eastern coast. Two groups, one the "sea people" and the other the "land people," were pitted against each other. The former team protected the goal near the sea and kicked the ball toward the land; while the latter team protected the landward goal and kicked toward the sea. The game was played with a stuffed leather ball called "aqsaq." Each team tried to keep the ball away from its own goal, which could be ten miles from the opponent's goal (Rasmussen, 1931; VanStone, 1962).

Little is known of the beginnings of Canadian ice hockey, but the game has retained the rough and tumble characteristics of the earlier British versions of stick ball games. Ice hockey appears to have been "invented" by Her Majesty's Royal Canadian Rifles unit of the Imperial Army, whose members played a crude kind of hockey game on the ice behind their barracks in Kingston, Canada, where "shinny," a sort of field hockey, had been played since the 1830s (Considine, 1982, p. 213). According to Considine, J.G.A. Creighton, as a student at McGill University in Montreal duiing the late 1870s, organized a game he had first tried in his native Halifax. Divided into two teams of thirty players each, Creighton's McGill classmates took part in what is widely regarded as the first rule-structured ice hockey game. As an immediate success, students from other schools adopted the new sport as an excellent outdoor game which could be played throughout Canada's long chilly winters. Players clamped skating blades on their shoes, wrapped magazines around their legs for shin pads, and borrowed field hockey sticks to hit a ball or some similar object between the goals, two poles stuck in the ice at each end of the playing area. The area was surrounded by one-foot high boards to keep the "puck" in play. By the 1880s other colleges had teams. By 1885, the first league was started at Kingston with Queen's University, Royal Military College, Kingston Athletics and Kingston Hockey Club. The rules stated that no more than seven players could be on the ice at any one time per team. The game was spread by the Canadian servicemen who moved to different posts over Canada. During the last two decades of the 1800s several amateur hockey leagues were formed in Canada, one of which was the Amateur Hockey Association in 1885, which later became the Canadian Amateur Hockey League in 1899. The famous Stanley Cup, donated by Canadian Governor General Frederick Arthur, Lord Stanley of Preston, was awarded for the first time in 1893 to the "best amateur team in Canada," the Montreal A.A.A.

According to Considine (1982) ice hockey rivalled lacrosse as the national sport by the 1890s. In 1893 ice hockey was introduced to the United States, and by 1896 the first hockey league was formed in the United States. Interestingly, in 1903 the first professional ice hockey team, the Portage Lakers of Houghton, Michigan, consisting of Canadian players, was organized in the United States. By 1904 the International Professional Hockey League was organized. In 1908 Canada's first professional hockey team, the Ontario Professional Hockey League, was formed. According to Considine, another professional league was formed in 1910, the five-team National Hockey Association, including the Montreal Canadiens, the oldest professional hockey team still in existence. In 1911 the Pacific Coast Hockey Association began. By 1917 in a strategy move, the National Hockey League was created by five out of the six teams of the National Hockey Association. In the 1920s the NHL became an international league by adding several United States teams, thus creating two leagues.

For over a century, ice hockey has continued to grow in both Canada and the United States; USSR has rivaled North America in fervor. One only need to recall the great rivalry between Canada and USSR with the Soviets controlling every Olympic and international competition since 1962. Beginning in 1972 this rivalry continued on the professional level with the "Summit Series" between the NHL All-Stars called "Team Canada" and USSR's national team. One remembers how the United States in 1960 Winter Olympics managed to defeat Russia and Canada for the gold medal and when in the 1980 Winter Olympics the United States "schoolboy" team defeated the Soviet team for the gold medal.

Since the turn of the century, professional hockey greats have captivated the hearts and imagination of hockey aficionados. In the following pages of this book you will see several famous names. Gordie Howe, who electrified the sporting public with his skill for thirty-two years, from 1946 to 1987 – and the more recent miracle-worker Wayne Gretzky, who in his first year (1979-80) led the National Hockey League with 86 assists and later set a new NHL record for goals? Jacques Plante, who is almost synonymous with the Montreal Canadiens' 1956-1960 possession of the Stanley Cup? Bobby Hull, sometimes called the "golden jet," who in the 1960s was hockey's greatest attraction?

The old timers will remember his ominous unpredictable 110 mph slap shot. Remember Bobby Orr, whose career ended in 1978 by knee injuries and who was probably the greatest defenseman in the history of ice hockey and maybe hockey's greatest player? Other players probably come to mind. One is Ken Dryden (1984) of the 196Os-70s Montreal Canadiens, whose excellent book, *The* Game, provides in retrospect extreme insight into the life and world of a hockey player. One could go on and on, but let's get to the important part of this book, the hockey phrases themselves.

References Cited

Avercamp, Hendrick, 1625. The Scene on the Ice Near a Town. Oil Painting on Oak, 58 cm by 89.8 cm. Netherlands.

Breughel, Peter. 1565. January: The Return of the Hunters. Oil on oak panel. 117 cm by 162 cm. Vienna: Kunst Historisches Museum.

Charlevois, Pierre de. 1761. *Journal of a Voyage to North* America, Vol. 3. London: R. & J. Dodsley.

Cheska, Alice Taylor, 1981. Games of the Native North Americans. In Gunther Luschen and George H. Sage (eds.) *Handbook of Social Science of Sport*. Champaign, IL: Stipes Publishing Company, pp. 4977.

Considine, Tim. 1982. *The Language of Sport*. New York, NY. World Almanac Publications.

Culin, Stewart. 1907. *Games of North American Indians*. Twenty-fourth Annual Report, Bureau of American Ethnology. Washington, D.C.: Government Printing Office.

Dryden, Ken. 1984. *The Game*. Toronto: Totem Books.

Gini, Corrida. 1939. Rural Ritual Games in Libya. *Rural Sociology*, 4: pp. 283-299.

Henderson, Robert W 1947. *Ball, Bat, and Bishop. NY*. Rockport Press, Inc. Republished by Gale Research Company, Book Tower, Detroit, 1974.

Nordenskiold, E. 1910. Spiele und Spielsachen im Gran Chaco und in Nordamerika. *Zeitschrift fur Ethnologie* 42, pp. 427-433.

Moss, Peter. 1962. *Sports and Pastimes through the Ages*. NY.. Areo Publishing Co. Inc.

Nelson, E.W. 1899. *The Eskimo About the Bering Strait*. Eighteenth Annual Report of the Bureau of American Ethnology: Part I. 1896-1897. Washington, DC: Government Printing Offlce.

Rasmussen, Knud. 1931. *The Netsilik Eskimos: Report of the Fifth Thule Expedition, 1921-1924*. Volume 8: Number 1-2. Copenhagen: Gyldendalske Boghandle, Nordisk Forlag.

Simri, Uriel. 1968. The Religious and Magical Function of Ball Games in Various Cultures. *Proceedings, First* International Seminar on the History of Physical Education and Sport. Netanya, Israel: Wingate Institute of Physical Education, pp. 2-1-220.

Smith, Jerald C. 1972. The Native American Ball Games. In Maria Hart (ed.) *Sport in the SocioCultural Process*. Dubuque, Iowa: Wm. C. Brown, pp. 346-358.

VanStone, J.W 1962. *Point Hope: An Eskimo Village in Transition*, Seattle: University of Washington Press.

Westermarck, E.A. 1926. *Ritual and Belief in Morocco*. Vol. 2, pp. 2

Alyce Cheska is, with Kendall Blanchard, author of *The Anthropology of Sport*. Boston: Bergin and Garvey, 1985.

Author's note: Because Quebec is one of hockey's traditional homes, this book has included a number of French phrases which have become part of hockey lore. These entries have been indicated by a boldface **(Fr)**.

1. What it is

We know that hockey is where we live,
where we can best meet and overcome pain
and wrong and death.
Life is just a place where we spend time between games.
— Fred Shero, quoted in Roy MacGregor, *The Last Season*

ball hockey – hockey played with a ball rather than a puck and with players wearing sneakers rather than skates, on street or ice. "Ball hockey is to hockey as stick-ball is to baseball, or one-on-one to basketball." R. Holcomb. Peter Chipman of Winnipeg, who played later for Navy teams in 1950s international competition ashore (in Japan, especially), remembers that moccasins rather than sneakers gave more slide, and that the tennis ball froze. This game is also played with a large soft foam rubber ball, which does not slide as well in light snow, but allows slapshots which aren't dangerous to the goalie.

bandy – according to Kendall Blanchard and Alyce Cheska *(The Anthropology of Sport,* Bergin and Garvey, 1985), "an early form of hockey in which the club was

called a **bandy.**" (p. 16) "Don't bandy words with me," in general use in the language, charges that the other person is playing, not serious.

boot hockey – another name for **street hockey, pond hockey, shinny.**

broomball – a game related to hockey, played on ice, but by players wearing tennis shoes, using as a puck a big ball and as a stick, a broom cut off short and the bristles dipped in paint to harden them.

Chinese hockey – shinny game, with no goalie, the nets turned backwards, scoring done by caroming off the boards. (Sudbury, 1950s, '60s).

grass hockey – British Columbia term for what is known elsewhere as "field hockey."

hockey – according to one widely known story, the word comes from an Indian word "ho ghee," (Tim Considine, The Language of Sport, p. 213) or "ha-ki" (Stephen Scriver, *The All-Star Poet*, Thunder Creek Publishing Cooperative, Box 239, Sub. No. 1, Moose Jaw, Sask., S6H 5V0), both meaning "it hurts." According to the Oxford English Dictionary, "(origin uncertain; but the analogy of many other games makes it likely that the name originally belonged to the hooked stick. Old French 'hoquet,''shepherd's staff, crook,' suits form and sense, but connecting links are wanting)." The OED cites a 1527 occurrence: "The horlinge of the litill balle with hockie sticks or staves." - Galway, Stat. in 10th Rep. Hist. Mss. Comm.

Not long thereafter, the secretary to Thomas A. Becket records, "When the great feene is frozen young men play upon the yee. Some tye bones to their feets and shoving themselves by a little picked staffe, doe slide as swiftly as an arrow out of a cross bow. Sometimes two runne together with poles and one doth fall, not without hurt. Youth desirous of glorie, in this sport exerciseth itself against the time of warre." - pointed out by Doug Beardsley, *Country on Ice, p.* 57.

horse hockey – hockey played with **horseballs** or **horse pucks.**

old time hockey – ambiguous term which means at different times "rough, tough hockey" and at others good, clean, energetic hockey." "Whaddya mean I knocked you down? Just old time hockey." Jean

Beliveau: "Fast skating, sharp passing, smart, clean defensive play, that's hockey."

pond hockey, pond skating – an ambiguous term which describes the outdoor situation where many players formerly learned skills. The organization of the game, the formations used, were loose; one did not play a strict position, but much skill was learned. Bob Richardson, an assistant coach at Boston University, has used the term and described its connotations: "One reason for the lack of good puckhandlers is that the number of kids who go pond skating seems to have diminished with the advent of indoor rinks. You can't fire the puck ahead or take slapshots on the pond. It takes' too long to find the lost pucks in the snow, or it is too far to chase it from one end of the pond to the other. So to keep the game moving you have to handle the puck and make well thought out stick to stick passes."
– "Stickhandling," *Hockey USA*, March 26, 1986.

raggedy hockey – hockey in which nothing much is happening. See also RAGGING THE PUCK.

ricket – according to Bill Fitsell, "a form of shinny introduced by British troops in Halifax, Nova Scotia" by 1842. The name came from the "rickets," "stones about as large as cobblestones" ..."placed three or four feet apart and frozen to the ice" to serve as goal and were placed at right angles to the length of the playing surface. An ancestor game of hockey, "ricket" allowed forward passing.

road hockey – "a simple variation of ice hockey played in the street by children using hockey sticks and a tennis ball," according to the Funk and Wagnalls Standard College Dictionary, Canadian edition, quoted by John Kalbfleisch in "Could You Say That in Canadian, Please?" *Weekend Magazine*, October 16, 1976. Kalbfleisch goes on to comment, "We often didn't have tennis balls. No, sir, it was nothing but road apples then... "

roller hockey – played in New York and no doubt other U. S. cities of the northeast, using a puck, on roller skates fitted with a special rubber bumper, for quick stopping. Play takes place on the street, of course, not on ice, and usually at a dead-end.

shinny – pickup hockey game without full protective equipment, probably named for the battering the players' shins suffer. Andy O'Brien records Jean Beliveau's belief that shinny teaches stickhandling: "Until then (Junior A), he had known only shinny hockey on a crowded rink where he had to stickhandle like crazy for any puck time." - *Superstars,*. p. 68.
According to Doug Beardsley, "among the native Wichita [Indians], the first man, whose name was Darkness, was guided to the Light by the flight of a shinny ball"; in a West Coast tale, "the face of Wildcat is smashed into its present shape by a shinny stick." He identifies Scotland as the source of the word "to depict the whack of the stick against the shin," but also says that Iroquois and Algonquin claim the original naming, with the same explanation of the sound. *(Country on Ice*, pp. 39-41.)

soul hockey – "brilliance, applied instinct, flashes - surprises." – from Sean Kelly, "The Canadiens and Soul Hockey," *New York Times* (Sunday, April 9, 1978), Sec. 5, p. 2.

2. Who is it?

PEOPLE, TEAMS, ROLES, JOBS, POSITIONS, LINES

the Arenas – first name of the Toronto Maple Leafs, from 1917 to 1919. See also **St. Patricks.**

Army – nickname of George Armstrong, of the Maple Leafs. See also **chief.**

backliner – defenseman. See also **blueliner.**

Battleship – nickname of Bob Kelley, Pittsburgh Penguins, 1970s. Also known as the **Hound Dog.** The name Battleship may derive from his skating skill: "moves in straight lines, turns like a battleship." See **bad wheels.** It has also been suggested that he got the name because he fought a lot.

the Bear – nickname of Tim Horton, Toronto and Philadelphia, who never fought but put opposing players in bear hugs.

the Best – nickname for Mario Lemieux, Pittsburgh Penguins, according to Doug Beardsley.

Big Bird – nickname of Larry Robinson of the Canadiens. According to Ken Dryden, the source of the nickname is his "snarl of curly hair." (p. 6)

Big Three S line – Nels (Ole Poison) Steward, "Uncle Hooley" Smith, and Babe Siebert, of the Montreal Maroons. – Stan Fischler, *Amazing Trivia from the World of Hockey* (Penguin, 1983).

Big Train – nickname of Lionel Conacher, of the New York Americans in the late twenties and the Montreal Maroons in the early thirties. He was a standout football player as well.

bird-dogs – In western Canada, "local part-time scouts [who] would tip a pro club or a college to come and see anyone who showed high promise." – from Scott Young's *Scrubs on Skates* (McClelland and Stewart, 1952, 1985).

the **Black Cat of Chicoutimi** – nickname of Johnny Gagnon, who played on a line with Morenz and Joliat and only weighed 140 pounds, according to Doug Beardsley, *Country on Ice.*

blender – "he's a real blender along the boards." – a player who chops the ice around the puck in a desperate attempt to either gain or retain control of the play. See also **eggbeater.**

bleu-blanc-rouge (Fr) – the colours of the Montréal Canadiens, in French. This phrase is also used in English, along with "the red-white-and-blue of the Montreal Canadiens." (See Sheila Fischman's translation of Roch Carrier's "The Hockey Sweater" [1979], and Goyens and Turowetz' Lions *in Winter* [1986]). The different word orders suggest the dual cultural heritage of the Canadiens, as in French the colours are given in the order associated with the French flag, the *tricolore*, and in English, in the order normally used to describe the U.S. flag, the Stars and Stripes.

Bleuet Bionique (Fr) – "the bionic blueberry," nickname of Mario Tremblay, Pittsburgh Penguins.

blueliner – defenseman. See also **backliner.**

buteur (Fr) – European word for "scorer." (Dallaire) See also **marqueur.**

Broadstreet Bullies – nickname of the Philadelphia Flyers in the 1970s. Broad Street, a main street in downtown Philadelphia, on which old City Hall is located, came to be identified with street violence as it was the territory for which rival street gangs fought.

Bronco – nickname of Joseph Horvath.

Busher – nickname of Floyd Curry, Canadiens, late '40s, early '50s.

the Canadien Comet – one of the many nicknames of Howie Morenz, who played **for** Montreal most of his brilliant career. See also **Mitchell Meteor, Stratford Streak, Swift Swiss.**

the Canard – nickname of Rejean Houle, Canadiens, 1969.

Cannie – nickname of Larry Playfair, Buffalo.

Captain Crunch – nickname of Gilles Marotte (Los Angeles) according to Dryden, "a thunderous bodychecker. "

Causeway Street Demolition Club – an old nickname for the Boston Bruins, emphasizing their working-class cultural identification with the Boston fans.

CBC line – Cullen, Barlow, Cullen of the St.Catherines, Ont., Teepees.

Cement Hands – nickname of Chris Nilan, when with the Canadiens, "cause he's a real bruiser."

Cement Head – nickname of Dave Semenko.

cerbère (Fr)– goalie, from "Cerberus," legendary classical guardian of the gates of Hell. (Robinson & Smith) As he was a dog, Cerberus adds (in French only) to the goalie mystique and reputation as an eccentric, moody, unpredictable player. See **ghoulie.**

CH – the logo of the Montreal Canadiens, inscribed at mid-rink of the Forum in red and blue. Explained by an anglophone (before 1976) as meaning "center hice," the way the Quebecois identify the spot where the logo appears on the rink surface. In fact one Quebecois gloss of this symbol is that it stands for "p'tit criss d'hostie," ("tiny Christ of the Host" – many French Canadian swear words come from Catholic rites) an oath uttered by Canadiens' fans when opposing teams score a goal. "Club de Hockey Canadien" is the official explanation, with one alternative given as "Canadiens Habitants."

Chicago Scraphawks – derogatory nickname for the Chicago Black Hawks.

the Chicoutimi Cucumber – nickname of Georges Vezina.

the Chief – nickname of George Armstrong, Maple Leafs, '50s-'60s. Also known as **Army,** he was the first Indian player in the NHL.

the China Wall – Johnny Bower, Toronto: "he stopped everything."

Clear the Track – nickname of Eddie Shack, Guelph Biltmores, Toronto Maple Leafs.

Clobber, Big Bobby – caricature stupid hockey player in skits by Toronto's Royal Canadian Air Farce, radio satirical skit team. It has been suggested that the name was chosen to echo "Bobby Clarke," notoriously rough player for the Philadelphia Flyers (see **Broadstreet bullies**).

Cyclone – nickname of Fred Taylor, Renfrew Creamery Kings, 1910-11, later with the Vancouver Millionaires.

le **Demon Blond (Fr)** – nickname for Guy Lafleur, according to Goyens and Turowetz, Lions *in* Winter.

the Edmonton Express – Eddie Shore, who came from the Western Canada League to Boston and played from the late 'twenties to 1940.

Eggbeater – nickname of Bert Olmstead, 1950s Canadien, for his "style of play in the corners. He would lift someone's stick, an effective legal manoeuvre, often resulting in the opponent fanning on the shot, or simply a steal." – from Robert Dickson. Olmstead's nickname is only one application of a term generally used for anyone who rapidly chops the ice with his stick when at close quarters in the corners, making him dangerous to any other player around. "He pulls an eggbeater whenever he gets in the corner!" "A real eggbeater" ... "A real blender in there." Dana Johnson, who played in the Bruins farm system and in West Germany, points out that "eggbeaters" are often players who can't **cradle** the puck, so they smack the ice repeatedly on both sides of it; he says the motion is also called "**to kill a snake**."

enforcer – a player whose main duty is to use brute strength and ruthlessness instead of skill. A **hatchetman**. Of his own career, Schultz *(Confessions of a Hockey Enforcer*, p. 13 1), says, "Even if I wanted to go straight, I said to myself, I couldn't: there were too many enforcers around the league looking to take me on and prove they were number one."

fireplug – short, stocky player, usually a defenceman, e.g. Léo Boivin, Bruins.

the **Flower** – Guy Lafleur, right winger of the Montreal Canadiens, 1971-1984.

Flower Power – nickname of Guy Lafleur. See also le **demon blond.**
the Flying Forts – Gus Bodnar, Norman (Bud) Poile, Gaye Stewart, three players for Toronto 1945-47, then Chicago Black Hawks, so named because all three were from Fort William, Ontario. – from Stan Fischler, *Amazing Trivia from the World of Hockey* (Penguin, 1983), p. 19.

the Flying Frenchmen – the Canadiens.

the Franchise – first a nickname for Gretzky: "Who is that with two goals and three assists? Just the Franchise, that's all." But by the winter of 1989-90, Pat Lafontaine, a brilliant young Canadien traded to the New York Islanders, was also known by this nickname. Therefore, a **franchise player** is a key player, a sparkplug, often a center, especially on a team where this single player's loss, through injury or trade, would mean the loss of the franchise. This somewhat hyperbolic term is shared with basketball, where it has the same sense.

Freddie Charles – "future considerations," as in "I've just been traded for Freddie Charles," (M. Farber, "F-Word Players Don't Say," Montreal *Gazette.*

French connection – Maurice "Rocket" Richard, center, and his line, of the Montreal Canadiens.

Gallery Gods – "fans who were maniacs but lively" according to Carol Smith, in George Plimpton, *Open Net*, New York: WW Norton, 1985, p. 220.

gamer – "an emotional player, a gamer, a shadow, so-and-so slowing down Messier." – John Allemang, "Name that goon," Word Play column in Montréal *Gazette, 1989.*

ghoulies – term applied to goalies, according to Dryden, because they tend to be "sensitive and moody." – p. 118. Also, many goalies mention how crazy they must be to stand in the path of the fast-moving puck. "He's seen more rubber than a dead skunk on the 401" – said of an old goalie, with reference to the long, straight, boring highway between Quebec and Toronto.

the **Giant Redwood** – Terry O'Reilly's nickname for Larry Robinson, Canadiens.

les Glorieux(Fr) – nickname for the Montreal Canadiens, "the glorious ones," the oldest professional hockey team still in existence in the world, and for many years the undisputed champions. It has been suggested that in their bad years, the Canadiens may be called les Glorieux in irony, but another of their names, les Saints Flannels (which see) is never used in anything but praise.

goldie – goalie, **ghoulie.** Perhaps because he is so valuable to the team.

Golden Jet – nickname of Bobby Hull, for his speed and yellow hair.

goon coach – after the 1984 playoff series in which Quebec eliminated the Buffalo Sabres, Buffalo coach Scotty Bowman called Quebec Nordiques coach Michel Bergeron a "goon coach" for his use of enforcer Jimmy Mann *(Globe and* Mail, October 26, 1985, page D3).

goons – a team which relies more on its players' size, strength, and vicious, dirty techniques. Such a team may be recognized by the odd Flyers sweater, worn by a player whose heroes are the Philadelphia Flyers in the late seventies, known as the **Broadstreet bullies** (which see). Also known as **ice thugs** (see George Plimpton, *Open Net*, New York: WW Norton, 1985, p. 95).

the Great One – Wayne Gretzky, formerly of the Edmonton Oilers, then an LA King, and in 1996, a member of the St. Louis Blues. Audrey Bakewell, a skating instructor who has worked with the Edmonton Oilers, says Gretzky can "skate from the hips down and play hockey from the hips up." – Kenneth Whyte, in "Nobody's Fifteen Feet Tall," *Saturday Night*, Jan.-Feb. 1990.

grinders – an ambiguous term, generally negative. It can refer to "solid defencemen," as Rod Langway, Washington Capitals defence-man does in Montreal Gazette February 12, 1985: "We've got some grinders this year, guys who'll be checking up and down the wings. I think the game is going to go that way." But generally, like "journey-man," in hockey it carries the sense of a player or a team without flash and brilliance, a "grinding, boring, defensive club," as Lawrence Martin says the Canadiens may become (*Gazette*, November, 1984) or Team Canada against a brilliantly offensive Soviet team. In the positive sense, it means "relentless, diligent, hard-working."

le gros Bill (Fr) – Jean Beliveau.

gros canon(Fr) – big gun, top scorer. See **triggerman, boulet, sniper.**

Gump – nickname of Lorne Worsley, Canadiens goalie. Also GUM-PER. It has been suggested that the nickname came from his early years, from Ash Avenue, the Point (Point St. Charles) in Montreal. In fact, Ronald Sutherland, of the University of Sherbrooke, who "once —scored two goals on him," says that the nickname came from his being grumpy, hence originally it was "the Gumper."

Habs – short for "Habitants," the Montreal Canadiens. The word, from French, means "those **who** live here," though always with a rural connotation, "the farmers."

hacker – a dirty, rough hockey player. The term suggests the use of slashing, barbarian tactics, stickswinging, etc.

the Hammer – nickname of Dave Schultz, enforcer of the **Broadstreet Bullies.**

Hinky – nickname of Billy Harris of the Maple Leafs.

homers – see entry under "How to."

hoser – this word, which has been spread across North America by the comedy team of Bob and Doug Mackenzie as a sort of gentle kidding insult, may have lost in its generalized popularity its origins. Quinn McIlhone, author of *Trade Rumours*, a novel about hockey published in 1985 by McClelland and Stewart, has pointed out that it probably came from the unofficial job title of the rink rat who watered the ice, he thinks in Ontario, to make it smooth, on outdoor rinks.

Howie – locker room nickname for Courtnall, "because of his shot" (M. Farber, Montreal *Gazette*). See **howitzer** in "What is That" section.

Industrial Hockey League – a league of nonprofessional players sponsored by a company. The term enters popular hockey to describe one's suspicions that players who have shown up aren't just off the street, but experienced and skilled – "they look like they're from an Industrial Hockey League."

the **Invisible** – another nickname for Wayne Gretzky.

Izzy – nickname of Larry Goodenough, who played briefly for Philadelphia and Vancouver.

Jake the Snake – nickname of Jacques Plante, Canadiens goalie, the first goalie to make a practice of skating out from the crease to intercept shots and disrupt the attack. This nickname is of course a piece of rhyming slang, like "make and break," the name of a type of old marine motor in the Maritimes.
Plante is also remembered for being the first goalie to wear a mask. Doug Beardsley tells the story best:

On November 1, 1959, Jacques Plante went to the Canadiens' dressing room after being hit by a shot, and returned wearing a mask. Plante had a long history of playing with masks, ... in baseball and lacrosse. He'd experimented with several masks, but only in practise, until that night Ranger great Andy Bathgate, parked directly in front of the crease, lifted a drive that almost tore Plante's nose from his face. When the injured netminder returned to the game sporting one of his practise masks, Coach Toe Blake was not amused. Blake felt that a goalie's reflexes would be affected because he'd relax a little and get too comfortable. But Plante was a great goaltender. When the Habs won 11 games in a row with the masked man in the cage – and won the Stanley Cup in 8 straight later the same year Blake had nothing but praise for his masked marvel.
– from *Country on Ice*, p. 170

the keeper – the goaltender.

the Kid line – Joe Primeau, **Harvey (Busher) Jackson,** Charlie (Big Bomber) Conacher, Toronto, 30s.

KLM line – famous Soviet line of Krutov, Larianov, and Makarov, all of whom were drafted by the hapless Vancouver Canucks in the dying rounds of a hopeless draft.

Knuckles – name given to Chris Nilan of the Rangers by Don Cherry "for real hard-hitting fights."

the Kraut line – Milt Schmidt, Woody Dumart, Bobby Bauer of Boston Bruins. "During World War II, they were renamed the Kitchener Kids, for fairly obvious reasons. (Personal note: until 1914, Kitchener was Berlin, Ontario.") – from Robert Dickson, Departement de littérature francais, Laurentian University, Sudbury, Ontario.

Lamplighter – nickname of Hector "Toe" Blake. The use of the old-fashioned word "lamp" for "light bulb" suggests the age of this synonym for "goal-scorer": when a goal is scored, a light bulb behind the goal comes on. His other nickname, "Toe," may be a short form of "Ecto,' " a Québécois pronunciation of "Hector."

loafer – also known as the "floater" – a forward who waits for a forward pass between his own blue line and the red line. Frank Mahovlich has been said to have been good at this.

Lunch Pail A.C. – Don Cherry's name for the "tough, hardworking, semiskilled core of the 1980s Bruins," according to Dryden.

Mad Dog Kelly – nickname for Robert James Kelly, the "Hound Dog," a player for Philadelphia Flyers, and Washington Capitols who was known as a **"digger"** or **"scrapper"** (which see) for his expertise at extracting the puck from tangles or players up against the boards behind and to the side of the net.

mighty Atom – nickname of Aurèle Joliat, diminutive Canadiens player of the 1920s. According to Goyens and Turowetz (Lions *in Winter*) he weighed 135 pounds! (1986: 38)

Mitchell Meteor – one of several nicknames of Howie Morenz, great 1930s Canadien. He was from Mitchell, Ontario. See also Stratford, Streak, Canadien Comet, Swift Swiss.

Moose – nickname of Elmer Vasko, Chicago Black Hawks 1956-66, then Minnesota North Stars.

the **MOST** – Gordie Howe "has been tagged 'the Most,' which is the only nickname that really fits a player who created a list of records as long as your arm. Among them: Most seasons played (25), most regular-season games (1687), most Hart Trophies (6), most Art Ross Trophies (6), most career goals in regular season play (786), and most selections to the NHL All-Star teams (21). – Andy O'Brien, *Superstars*.

Motor City Six – name given to the Detroit Red Wings between 1951-1954, when their star player Gordie Howe led them to four straight Stanley Cups.

Mr. Elbow – Gordie Howe.

Mr. Goalie – according to Doug Beardsley, nickname for Glenn Hall. Even he had "a queasy stomach" and did "more than once leave the ice suddenly during a stoppage in play, returning, without explanation, a few minutes later." - *Country on Ice*, p. 173.

net hanger – a player who hangs around the net, waiting for easy goals. Of course, while the play is in his zone, he waits around the center line. According to Peter Gzowski, GOAL SUCKER is another term for this kind of player. See also **cherrypicker.**

netminder – a term for goalie. – Howard Liss, *Hockey Talk for Beginners.*

Newsy – nickname of Edouard Lalonde, of the Canadiens, from the beginning until his trade to the Saskatoon Sheiks in the early 1920s. According to Stan Fischler, the nickname referred to "his habit of stuffing newspapers into his sweater, all lumps and bumps" because "they played in a frigid former granary." *Amazing Trivia from the World of Hockey,* p. 41. But the *Pocket Hockey Encyclopedia* (BVB Research: Penguin Press, 1972) has it that he was an apprentice printer before he played hockey professionally, and "came to hockey with printers' ink on his hands."

Nitro line – Wayne Cashman, Phil Esposito, Ken Hodge, for the Boston Bruins during the time Orr was defenceman with the team.

No Name League – a pickup league in Boston so old that over ten years ago a Boston newspaper reporter did a story on it. He came to a game, met the players in the dressing room, and after a while began to ask someone for people's names. He was surprised to discover that no one knew anyone else's last name; everybody knew everyone else by a first name or nickname. So he dubbed it the No Name League, and it stuck.

Ole Poison – nickname of Nels Stewart, Montreal Maroons, who held the NHL scoring record of 324 until it was broken by Rocket Richard.

penalty killer – "Eric Nestorenko was a strong penalty killer, his roaming style adapted to breaking up rushes before they started. He was an especially great penalty killer when his team was two men short. Swooping in upon the puck carrier, harassing him with his long, gangling reach, retreating to intercept passes, ragging the puck for a few seconds before shovelling it deep into the opposition's zone, he was able to reduce the most disciplined power play to a rabble." – Hanford Woods, "The Drubbing of Nestorenko," in George Bowering's *Great Canadian Sports Stories* (Oberon, 1979).

Pie – nickname of John McKenzie, Boston Bruins, 1960s and 70s. The name was given by Gerry Melnyk, Buffalo, "because he thought my round face looked like a pie." – Quoted in Andy O'Brien, *Superstars*, p. 162.

playmaker – a player who gets assists, setting up plays which lead to goals.

Pocket Rocket – nickname of Henri Richard, after his elder brother Maurice "Rocket" Richard, Montreal Canadiens. See also **Vest Pocket Rocket.**

pointman – defenseman who waits at the point.

Pointu – nickname of Guy LaPointe, Montreal Canadiens after 1968.

the Police – common term for John Ferguson, during his days with the Montreal Canadiens.

policeman – the role on a team played by someone who energetically and efficiently stops fights, redresses wrongs, etc., according to Tiger Williams.

the Production line – Gordie Howe, Sid Abel, and Ted Lindsay of the Detroit Red Wings in the late 1940s and early 1950s.

Puck-goes-inski – nickname for Steve Buzinski, New York Ranger goalie in 1942 who stood in a wide stance and was said to be bowlegged. – Stan Fischler, *Amazing Trivia* ..., p. 125.

Punch – nickname of George Imlach, Canadiens coach, Toronto and Buffalo coach during the Orr years.

Punch Line – Toe Blake, Elmer Lach, Rocket Richard (1940s) Canadiens, created by Dick Irvin, 1942.

the Rat – nickname of Ken Linseman, Toronto.

rink bunny – a young girl who waits around the rink for a date with the star player. – from Greg Tyler, Concordia University.

rink rat – kid who hangs around the hockey rink a lot.

Roadrunner – nickname of Yvan Cournoyer, Canadiens.

Rocket – nickname of Maurice Richard, Canadiens. According to Dick Irvin in *Now Back to You Dick*, the name was first applied by a teammate, Ray Getliffe, a defensive forward who "was never on the ice at the same time ... so he had a great ice-level view of him in action." Once, during a practice, he said, "That kid can take off just like a rocket. A few nights later during a game, Richard made a great play and Getliffe said to his mates on the bench, 'There he goes again, just like a rocket.' " So he was called by his nickname in the dressing room before it appeared in print.

les **Saints Flanelles(Fr)** – the Canadiens (for colours of the Habs). See also les **Glorieux.** Of course "flanelle" refers initially to the woolen underwear worn in winter.

Scarface – nickname of Ted Lindsay, Detroit, 1944-1965.

Scratch – nickname of Dave Ratchford, according to Doug Beardsley, because "he was constantly scratching himself." He goes on to say that Ratchford was "an excellent hockey player, a strong fierce-checking defenceman who used his butt as a block or bumper to stop the swiftest skater cold in his tracks." – *Country on Ice, p.* 74.

Seldom – nickname of Frank Beaton, New York Islanders, 1982-83. From Stan Fischler, Amazing *Trivia from the World of Hockey,* Penguin 1983, p. 24. Dana Johnson, who played in the Bruins farm system and in West Germany, recalls that he was also known by the nickname "Master."

the **Sheriff** – nickname of John Ferguson, Canadiens. For an explanation of the name, see Hanford Woods' story "The Drubbing of Nesterenko" in *Great Canadian Sports Stories* ed. George Bowering (Oberon, 1979). See also **policeman.**

sniper – hot scorer. See also **triggerman.**

chief **snowball thrower** – used to designate Brian McNeil, who as leading official of the National Hockey League, is in charge of deciding the penalties in cases involving major offenses, long suspensions, drug use, and so forth. – Peter Leney.

stickman – a player skilled at stickhandling? or a player who uses his stick on other players, a dirty player? The term is borrowed from hockey or baseball use and given quite a specific sexual meaning in the script for the movie "Last Tango in Paris."

the St. Patricks – name of the Toronto Maple Leafs from 1919 to 1927. See also **Arenas**.

Stratford Streak, Swift Swiss – one of the several nicknames of Howie Morenz, great Canadiens player of the 1930s. He was actually from Mitchell, Ontario, near Stratford. See also **Mitchell Meteor, Canadien Comet**.

SWOOP – "Swoop" Carleton.

Tasmanian Devil – nickname of Terry O'Reilly, Boston Bruin in the late 1970s.

Teeder – nickname of Ted Kennedy of the Maple Leafs.

Tiger – nickname of Dave Williams, Toronto, 1970s.

Tip-In – nickname of Sid Smith, Toronto Maple Leafs, according to Pagnucco, *SuperStars*.

the **Tunnel** – nickname of hot new player (1989-90) Pat Lafontaine, Canadiens, then traded to New York Islanders. Named for the Lafontaine Tunnel, which runs under the St. Lawrence River from Montreal to Longueil, on the South Shore.

the **Turkey** – nickname of Gerard Gallant of the Detroit Red Wings.

Uke Line – Uke for Ukrainian, this famous Boston Bruin line consisted of John Bucyk, Bronco Horvath, and Vic Stasiuk.

Uncle Hooley – nickname of Reginald Joseph Smith, a player from 1924 to 1941, with Ottawa, Montreal, Boston, and New York.

Vest Pocket Rocket – nickname for Claude Richard, brother of Rocket and Henri, the Rocket and the Pocket Rocket, who tried out for but didn't stick with the Habs.

Wild Bill – nickname of Ezinicki of the Maple Leafs.

Mr. Zero – nickname of Frankie Brimsek, goalie, Bruins, late 30s and early 40s. "Responsible for introducing the trapper glove... rather than the then traditional hockey goalie's gauntlet ... for catching pucks." – Stan Fischler, Amazing *Trivia from the World of hockey* (Penguin, 1983), p. 37.

3. Where?

PLACES

control of the **alleys** – the "alleys" are the parts of the ice along the **boards.** When the defense captures the puck after all shots along the boards, they have control of the alleys. – from Ian Ferguson.

aréna – "faulty expression," in French Canada, according to Dallaire, but nevertheless in use for "the place where hockey games occur." Also in use are **amphiglace, patinoire,** and palais des sports.However, patinathèque" and "patinodrome" refer, like "roulathèque," to places for "patin à roulettes(roller skating)." See also **dome, Homerdome.**

Beanpot Tournament – an annual set of matches played between longtime hockey rivals Boston College, Boston University, Harvard, and Northeastern University. The trophy is a beanpot, of course!

between the pipes – a goal!- the spot in front of the goal. "What position do
you play?" "Between the pipes!" See also **hit the pipe.**

cage (Fr) – the **goal** in French, and **in the cell** – playing goalie, "between the pipes," according to "Seaweed," a rookie goalie for the Brains, as quoted by George Plimpton, *Open Net*, New York: WW. Norton, 1985, p. 36. Another way to say this, for "old-time goalies," was "in the barrel," but "these days no self-respecting goaltender would say such a thing," because it was "a demeaning phrase." I suspect its connotations have been intensified by the widespread knowledge of an off-color joke about lumber camps in which the punch line refers to being in a barrel to perform sexual services for the men working there without women.

coast-to-coast – also known as **end-to-end,** this term is used when a player, usually a defenceman, starts a play or carries the puck from behind his own net, and moves the puck right into the other end, usually scoring a goal **or** assisting on one. "Orr took that one coast-to-coast for his second goal of the night!" – from Leslie Bairstow.

the crease – the area on the ice immediately in front of the net.

–dome – as a combining form, added to aggrandize, perhaps satirically, the name of the place where the **homers** play, e.g. as in Gaiterdome for Bishops University in Lennoxville, Quebec, and Stingerdome, for the home rink of the Concordia University college team. See **Homerdome, arena.**

get to Quebec – some idea of how much Quebec is hockey heaven may be gleaned from noticing the use of this phrase in Ken Dryden's second installment of Home Game, CBC-TV February 11, 1990. Boys describe arrival in Quebec City for the playoffs in municipal league hockey in tones of wonder (fans sometimes ask for the autograph of ll-year-old stars, in one case, leaning over the goal from the seats!) "When we got to Quebec... !!!"

the Gondola – Foster Hewitt's name for the broadcast booth at Maple Leaf Gardens, suspended high above the action. In a column in memory of Hewitt in the Montreal *Gazette* (April 23, 1985), Ted Blackman claims that Foster Hewitt's language was more colorful, better than that of Danny Gallivan despite the fact that "the only Canadian constituency Hewitt failed to capture was Montreal. He was to Canadiens' fans a Lord Ha-Ha or Tokyo Rose and viewed passionately as a Toronto **homer.**

Homerdome, Humperdome – two nicknames of the stadium in Minneapolis where the Twins, a baseball team, plays. "Humper" likely derives from "Hubert Humphrey," native son and politician; for the etymology of "Homerdome," see **homers.**

the open side – of the net. See LONG SIDE.

the point – spot just inside the blue line on each side of the rink where defensemen wait for possible shots on net and to keep the puck in the zone.

the short side – of the goalie, the side toward which he is closest to the goal-post. "And Hunter beats Penney on the short side!"

the slot – the area in front of the net between the two circles, on the ice surface. See also **crease.**

smoking section – just inside the blue line, hungry, large defensemen wait eagerly for the puck to drop back to the point so that they may smoke the puck hard toward the goal and anything in between. "Pass it back here, there's three of us in the smoking section and the net's wide open!"

the sweet spot – the goal, **or** the place from which one shoots a goal. "You've found the sweet **spot!**" – from George Bowering.

4. When?

THEN AND NOW: HOCKEY HISTORY IN TALK

after the skates go **blunt** – an expression, attribut,d to Ted Blackman of Montreal's radio station CJAD, to describe when someone goes into retirement from active professional play.

bobtailed hockey – derogatory term for the new kind of hockey played after 1912 when the position of "rover" was abolished, reducing the teams to six on a side, as they have remained since.

Boston Flu – a common disease suffered by many players on teams who had games coming up against the Boston Bruins when they were the team to beat. "A groin-pull, hamstring-pull, anything-pull to keep the fainthearted out of Boston and safely away from them." – Ken Dryden, *The Game*, p. 105.

Broadstreet shuffle – the **dance** so commonly engaged in on the ice, the fighting which was the trademark of the Philadelphia Flyers in the 1970s, the Broadstreet Bullies.

bully – verb, early term for what was later called the "face-off," with the additional requirement that the "facing centres ...alternately bang their sticks together before attempting to gain possession of the object." (Bill Fitsell, *Hockey's Captains, Colonels & Kings*.)

I don't care if he puts a **bucket on his head,** as long as he stops the puck – attributed to Frank Selke, general manager of the Canadiens, after Jacques Plante became the first goalie to wear a mask. There was some question whether the mask would interfere with the visibility of the puck, but Plante's goaltending quickly established its usefulness. – from Frank Pagnucco, *Heroes: Stars of hockey's Golden Era* (Prentice-Hall, 1985).

dent the twine – old way to say "score a goal."

Donutgate – derogatory name for the perceived crisis over violence in the LHN/NHL precipitated by the events of May 6 and 8, 1988. See "have another **donut you fat pig!**" Also known as **the great Donut caper.**

elbows as sharp as Gordie Howe's – hockey simile based on the technique and anatomy of Mr. Elbow.

Elmer – see entry under "Hockey Talking."

expansion team – a team in the National Hockey League other than the **Original Six,** i.e. Dallas Stars, Quebec Nordiques, Colorado Avalanche, Hartford Whalers, New Jersey Devils, etc., teams some of which were created when the league was expanded, and others taken into the league after the failure of the World Hockey Association.

firewagon hockey – a style of play in which speed is the most important factor, The Montreal Canadiens' game in the 1970s. Dryden says, "Speed is disorienting ... It robs an opponent of coordination and control, stripping away skills, breaking down systems, making even the simplest tasks seem difficult." *The* Game, (p. 39)

the GAG line – for Goal a Game, the line of Rod Gilbert, Vie Hadfield, and Jean Ratelle, New York Rangers, early 1970s. This trio was so successful that according to Andy O'Brien local sportswriters eventually dubbed them the TAG line, for Two Goals a Game (*Superstars: Hockey's Greatest Players*, Toronto: McGraw Hill Ryerson, 1973), p. 97.

gouret(Fr) – an early French Canadian word for "hockey." A 1914 text by Charles Daveluy proposes the word "gouret" for hockey, and a "glossary for gouret" appears in the *Dictionnaire du Bon Language* (the Dictionary of Proper Language) by the Abbé Etienne Blanchard, a well-known purist of that era. – Aléong

horseballs – frozen chunks of horse manure, collected from the street or road and used as pucks by kids. See also HORSE HOCKEY. Horseballs were used in the cities (horses pulled ice-wagons), in the West, and in the North, where the horseballs froze fast, until the fiffies. In the north, when it warmed up, they became "honeybags" for ball and other sports; but the term was something of a joke, as the frozen earth there makes septic systems impossible to dig; so plastic bags were used for toilets, then put out to freeze and be collected. These are known as "honeybags." In the west, there was a related term – "buffalo buns." Also known as **horse pucks.**

Hot Stove League – "Back when hockey was only done on radio on Saturday night, on CBC, there'd be a "Hot Stove League" between periods. There'd be four gents. In Montreal, or from Montreal, accompanying English language Canadiens' broadcasts, were Basil O'Meara and Elmer Ferguson, who wrote for the *Star* and *Herald*, I think." – R. Holcomb. See also **Bas** and **Elmer.** Names of other commentators on the Hot Stove League include of course Foster Hewitt, but also Wes McKnight, Jack Dennett, Harold Cotton, and Courtney (or Gordon?) Benson (who claimed, on CBC radio during the memorials to Foster Hewitt after his death April 20, 1985, to

48

have been kept a year in Camp Borden rather than being sent overseas to World War II, so he could do the Hot Stove League!)

hurley – an old Irish ground hockey game, which, together with ice-based versions called **bandy** (British), and **shinty** (Scottish), date from the 14th century and are ancestor games of hockey. "In an essay by Thomas Chandler Haliburton published in a British magazine called *Attache* in 1844, the early Canadian author of the Sam Slick tales describes a game of hurley played at King's Edgehill School (Windsor, N.S.) before his graduation in 1810, thus establishing securely the claim of Nova Scotia to be the origin of hockey in Canada, over rival claims by ffingston and Montreal. The 1875 Montreal game between McGill and Kingston was played by 'Halifax rules,' anyhow; and an earlier game in Kingston pitted an army garrison against the Halifax garrison (1855)." – Sandy Young, sports historian, Dalhousie University, in a lecture at King's, October 1988.

masks – According to Doug Beardsley, the first goalie to don a mask was Clint Benedict, "long-forgotten netminder for the Montreal Maroons in the 1920s, ... after his nose and cheekbones were shattered by a drive off the stick of Howie Morenz. Made of leather, the mask was strapped on and covered his forehead, nose, cheeks, and chin. Abandoning it after a single game because it obscured his vision, Benedict's career was later ended by another Morenz shot, this time to the throat." – *Country on Ice* - Jacques Plante (see **Jake the Snake**) was the first to wear one regularly.

Original Six – Between 1942/3 and 1966/7 the National Hockey League had six teams: Montreal, Toronto, Boston, New York, Detroit, and Chicago. Then came expansion, and the WHA, and things have never been the same again.

rover – a player who has to play on both offensive and defensive lines, or who does not play a particular position. Originally this word referred to a seventh player, a fourth forward who had no fixed position. When in 1912 the teams were reduced to six men each by the abolition of the post of rover, many fans didn't like it. See **bobtailed hockey.**

snowbankers – a tradition of the game of hockey, whereby progress in style of play was retarded, according to Clarence Campbell, then president of the NHL. "The boy becomes a man, the player a coach, a manager, a scout, a father; the game is passed on like tribal history, one voice, one mind. There was no bigger picture, no history in like games, in soccer or basketball, no parallel traditions in schools or universities, no critical mind, no oblique other eye to break the relentless continuum; there was simply no other way to play." – Dryden, p. 216. Dryden is describing the surprising fact that it took "more than fifty years for the forward pass to be introduced," in early years plays and rules recognizing only lateral and backward passing because territory gained by forward pass seemed "unearned." Thus play followed the puckcarrier strictly, and was much more unexciting.

Team Surfboard – nickname of the Los Angeles Kings, according to Goyens and Turowetz (1986:315). Also known as the Hollywood Cabana Club. Of this team, it has been said, "It's like in capitalism you have to have a lower class. In hockey, you have to have the L.A. Kings." And again, "in L.A., they don't know a hockey puck from a beach ball ... it's the Siberia of hockey." All of this was said before and repeated on the occasion of the trading of Wayne Gretzky to the Los Angeles Kings.

WHA – the World Hockey Association, a league created to compete with the National Hockey League. Upon its failure, some of its teams (Edmonton Oilers, Winnipeg Jets, Hartford – New England – Whalers, and the Quebec Nordiques) were taken into the N.H.L. as **expansion teams.**

Yellow Sunday – May 8, 1988; fourth game of Boston Bruins-New Jersey Devils Stanley Cup playoff, in which coach Schoenefeld, having obtained an injunction reversing his suspension for events following the previous game (see "Insults" section entry "Have another **DONUT, YOU FAT PIG"**), the officials refused to officiate. The game, delayed an hour, went on using three over-age referees in AHL jerseys (bright yellow). See Sandy Jenkins' book *Yellow Sunday.*

5. What is that?

THINGS

attaque à cinq – jeu de puissance(French), "power play." Literally "attack by five," because it is the coordinated attempt to score against a team which has a one-player disadvantage due to the absence from the ice of a penalized player. (Robinson & Smith)

balle – one of the many words in French for "the puck." (Aléong)

banana blade – "a stick with a pronounced curve in the blade to give better control of the puck when shooting." – Tim Considine, *The Language of Sport.* See also **big spoons** and **Winnipeg curve.** It is said that Bobby Hull's curved stick was the key to the legendary speed, 115 mph, of his slapshots. According to Howard Liss, originally much more pronounced, the stick's curve has been reduced by rules. He tells the story of the origin of the banana blade: "Stan Mikita, in practice, noticed that his shots were behaving strangely. The puck would dip down, sail up, or curve away. He saw that his stick's blade was cracked and bent." -*Hockey Talk for Beginners*, p. 14.

baton – Quebec term for hockey stick, known in Europe as **crosse.**

the Big Bamboo – the hockey stick, especially when used effectively (and not necessarily legally).

the Big Spoons – "the deep curved sticks of Bobby Hull, Andy Bathgate, and Stan Mikita," according to Gordie Howe. (p. 26)

the biscuit – the puck. "Put the biscuit in the basket!"

le biscuit(Fr) – the puck. (Aléong) "Donnez-moi l'biscuit, là!" "Put the biscuit in the basket!" According to Pierre Ladouceur, hockey writer for *La Presse*, used to designate the **bloqueur,** the goalie's big glove.

Blueline Fever – suffered by defensemen at times accord'ng to Goyens and Turowetz, Lions *in Winter* (1986:372).

the Board – "a piece of plywood cut at each corner and at its groin, hung from a crossbar to cover a net when a goalie is absent." – Ken Dryden, *The Game, p.* 6. From the world of back yard hockey.

ton **bois(Fr)** – "your stick." "Va cherchez ton bois!" ("go get your stick!" – de Shediac, N.B., d'apres André Richard).

boomer – a complimentary term for a hard, deadly slapshot. Probably the source of Montreal Canadiens' Boom-Boom Geoffrion's nickname.

box or box formation – penalty-killing defensive formation in which the four players remaining on the ice form a box in their own zone and attempt to keep the play outside of the slot and prevent any clear shots on their net.

brain bucket – slang term for the hockey helmet. Also used for motorcycle helmet (see Lewis Poteet and Jim Poteet's *Car and Motorcycle Slang).*

break – opening in a play.
  – a chance to score.
  – a play in which puckcarrier gets out ahead of other players and confronts the goalie one-on-one.

Broadstreet shuffle – see entry under "Dirty Tricks."

buggywhips – "skinny legs," from M. Farber, Montreal *Gazette*. See also **pistons, wheels, jets.**

bump and grind defense – "Lemaire, a smoothskating, two-way centre on those (Canadiens 1970s) championship teams, wasted little time implementing a **bump and grind** defensive system that rankled Guy Lafleur and Steve Shutt, the only stars who remained from the dynasty, which was epitomized by its firewagon offence." – Halifax *Chronicle-Herald*, June 30, 1985, p. 8. See **firewagon.**

bumping – "hard hitting," in classic understatement. Dick Irvin, using the word in the game that saw the return of Guy Lafleur in a New York Rangers uniform to the Forum, where he had played many seasons for the Canadiens, noted that there had been very little "bumping, if you could use that word." The latter phrase is a marker for a bit of special hockey talk to follow...

the cage – the net, not the penalty box. See **sin bin.** Consider also this use of the word: "In this case the mark against him is looks. Not pure enough to play out; admissible only if he keeps it all behind the cage," where it seems to mean "face-mask" but carries also the sense of "goal-crease." – from Roy MacGregor's The *Last Season*, p. 166.

the can – the jockstrap. From Stephen Scriver, *The All-Star Poet.*

caoutchouc(Fr) – "rubber," one of the terms used occasionally since 1900 for "the puck." – Aléong.

the catwalk – nickname for the Montreal Canadiens' broadcast booth at the Forum, as distinguished from the **gondola** of the Maple Leaf Gardens.

chandail (d'équipe)(Fr) – team jersey, sweater in North America. In Europe it is **maillot.** (Dallaire).

cheapskate – a greedy teammate who won't lend you any of his tape.
–- a crummy old skate that you would have to pay someone to take away at the skate exchange.
–- an inexpensive indoor pickup game. "You want to go for a cheap skate, only three dollars for a whole day of hockey."
–- an uneventful game which was not worth even putting your equipment on for. "Boy, what a cheap skate that was, eh?"

check league – in Boston, a league in which "hammering guys into the boards" is allowed is known as a "check league," one in which it is forbidden as a "no-check league." In Montreal, the same kinds of leagues are known, respectively, as "contact" and "not a contact" league.

checking line – a line of forwards who mainly play defensively. e.g. – Gainey, Carbonneau and Nilan of the Canadiens.

cheesecutters – beginners' skates, with two blades on each. "These skates are so dull, you'd be better off on cheesecutters." Also known as **bobskates**.

cherrypicker – another term for a guy who gets cheap goals, who waits at the center line for an easy shot when the puck's in his zone. See also **nethanger**. A term also used in basketball for the same sort of player.

contact league – Montreal term for a league in which hard checking is allowed. See also **check league**.

coquille -(Fr) "jock strap," athletic supporter. Literally: "shell," from the shape. See **also jockstrap**.

crochet(Fr) – poke check – 'With the stick close to the body and extended at full length, 'poking' the puck off the opponent's stick." –

Orr on Ice, p. 69. Like "tricoter," the word comes from women's crafts...

crosse(Fr) – European word for "Hockey Stick," bâton." (Dallaire)

disque(Fr) – the favorite word among the many possible choices for "the puck" of René Lecavalier, the first hockey announcer on Radio-Canada when French language broadcasts began in 1953 and the "father of Québécois hockey terminology." Despite his efforts, **rondelle** was and remains the primary, most often used word, but **disque** is still frequently heard, as are **balle, petite roulette, biscuit, puck, caoutchouc.** –Aléong.

filet(Fr) – the goal, the **but, cage.** Literally: the net. Compare English: to **dent the twine.** In Europe: **cage, goal.** (Dallaire)

five-hole – the opening between the goalie's legs. If you put one between the pads, and he doesn't close up in time to get it, you've scored in the five-hole! – from Leslie Bairstow. See also **the shed.** – also used in Doug Beardsley, *Country on Ice.*.

garbage goals – easy, cheap goals, scored by someone who doesn't deserve most of the credit, as someone else did the hard work.

garbage mitts – gloves used by western Canadian goalies, "padded for heavy duty by city workers," in outdoor ice hockey, according to Peter Gzowski, The *Game of Our Lives*, Toronto, McClelland and Stewart, 1983, p. 81. "Maritimers used their father's work gauntlets, with heavy leather up the wrists."

take the **gate,** get the **gate** – to be sent to the penalty box.

a **gathering of the clans** – ironic announcer's phrase for a fight, especially when teammates rush to join the two who started it.

gauntlet – the name often used in Eastern Canadian hockey for the hockey glove (as it is almost always known in the U.S.). The term is derived from very old terminology of armour, and from the French word for "glove," gant.

goal – fairly common word in French to describe the metal uprights with net at which players shoot the puck in order to score. Also known as the **cage**. The word also is in use as a verb: to **goaler(Fr)** is to "play in the goalie position," to **"jouer" goal.**

hang up the blades – retire.

hard stick – according to Howard Liss, "When one player passes to another, the receiving player's stick should 'give' somewhat ... 'Hard stick' means that the player receiving the pass is holding his stick so tightly and rigidly that it does not move back at all. That makes control of the puck difficult, and sometimes it bounces off the receiver's stick blade."

hat trick – a player's scoring three goals in one game. A term from cricket.

hockey cushion – an outdoor rink of natural ice on which hockey may be played.

hockey mums – that legion of mothers standing around dank arenas across the North on Saturday mornings.

hook – hold the opposing player back (illegally) with one's stick. Memorialized in Nancy Dowd's script for the movie Slap Shot in the figure of Dr. Hook, a particularly vicious player skilled with the stick-as-hook.

howitzer – a hard shot, according to M. Farber, Montreal *Gazette*. See also **Howie**.

iron lung – team name for the team bus, according to Tiger Williams.

it – in announcing, the word "it" almost always means the puck, and this use of the word is not explained. This use of the word makes the object so identified sound like the quarry, the prey, in hunting.

jackstrap(Fr) – the athletic supporter, or "jockstrap" in French. See also **coquille**.

jets – "legs." according to M. Farber, Montreal *Gazette*. See also **pistons, wheels**.

jill – female form of the jock cup, to protect the genitals. "It's a latex rubber-coated triangle worn the same way as a jock except it doesn't travel underneath quite so far ... also used in girls' lacrosse." Women also wear "shoulder pads... like the old defenceman's pads -longer in the front pecs and down almost to the bottom of the rib cage... with two hard cups on the front." – Becky Smith of Cape Breton, reported in Doug Beardsley, *Country on Ice*, p. 116-117.

joute(Fr) – despite its archaism (Dallaire), this word continues in use, echoing the medieval world of "jousts," and suggesting the truth that hockey is older than its formal history (1875...) as a North American organized sport. See Alyce Cheska's "Ice Hockey Then & Now" (appendix) for an account of the antiquity of stickball games, the class to which hockey belongs. To an English ear, in fact, much of the Quebecois terminology sounds wonderfully medieval: lances, gants, jousts, plastrons (hauberts), gauntlets.
Stanley Aléong has pointed out that around the turn of the century "Joute" was proposed as a corrective form for "game," i.e. to prevent the use of the English word, despite the medieval connotations of the

word in standard French. It has not yet, however, succeeded in this effort.

lancer frappé (Fr)- slapshot, Literally: a "struck," "thrown" or "hit" shot. (Robinson & Smith) The expression succeeds in usage despite the logical contradictions, which numerous French language purists have pointed out, inherent in the concept of something both hit and thrown at the same time!

maillot(Fr)- European word for **chandail (d'équipe)**, team jersey/sweater. (Dallaire)

marqueur(Fr) – Dallaire's suggested "correct" word for what most speakers know, in both languages, as "Scorer." (Aléong) The European word is **"buteur."**

paddle – the stick. "He lays the paddle down during the wraparound." –from Bill Fitsell.

palet (Fr)- European word for "puck," used alongside "puck" itself in European French. (Dallaire)

passe en diagonale(Fr) – cross-ice pass. In Europe, it is **transversale.** (Dallaire)

période(Fr) – "Period." In Europe it is **tiers-ter** s. See also **vingt** (Dallaire)

petite roulette(Fr) – very early term (1902) for **"puck," "rondelle."** Still in use occasionally, according to Aléong.

the pines – the bench. "He rode the pines a lot in his rookie season." – Tim Considine, *The Language of Sport.*

plaquage(Fr) – **mise échec(Fr)**, **"body-check."** (Dallaire) The French is much more colourful than the English: it means literally "plating." "Plaquage" is the standard French term in Europe. For a general pattern that describes the multiple synonym/"mismaster" phenomenon in usage of this and other key Québécois hockey terms, see the entry under **rondelle.**

plastron(Fr) – French term for breastplate, shirt-front, "dicky." The breast protector. The word is from Italian *piastrone*, "haubert," a medieval word.

puck – universal English name, even sometimes used in French, for the rubber disc over which players contend for control. The word is very old, having been in 1640 a verb, from Middle French, meaning to "poke," to "hit or strike." According to the Oxford English Dictionary, it became obsolete, except dialectal, but it may have been transmitted in slang through the Irish game of hurling, and may have originally come from Celtic, Teutonic, or Norse sources, where it may have meant a curved stick. It may have been transmitted through late Middle Dutch or German, and words closely related occur in Gaelic (puc – to push or shove) and Irish (poc – a blow, kick). On the current status of the French use of the word (in Québec) see Stanley Aléong's "Histoire du vocabulaire quebecois du hockey sur glace," *La Banque des Mots* (no. 20), 1980, pp. 195-210.

road apples – chunks of frozen or dried horse manure, used as pucks in **road hockey,** also called **horse hockey.**

rondelle(Fr) – "the little round thing," the puck. The leading, most frequently used term, despite the influence of René Lecavalier, who preferred **disque.** It first appeared in 1920, and soon became the word of choice, but its dominance has not completely ended all use of many synonyms: **balle, biscuit, disque, puck, caoutchouc, petite roulette** (Aléong). In Europe, the terms used are **palet** and **puck.** (Dallaire)

Stanley Aléong has observed that the paradoxical efect resulting from various efforts at linguistic purist correction of what were taken to be *expressions fautives* (erroneous expressions) is that contemporary language police are having to update the "proper French" expressions introduced correctively forty or more years ago. Thus for many common phenomena – the words for the puck, the words for **plaquage**, etc. – at least three waves of usage have appeared and no one wave has driven out all the others. "Proper French" itself has changed, particularly in Europe. The effect is to leave in use a range of multiple synonyms or vanant forms. We might call it the "mixmaster" effect.

One of the most amusing of these odd occurrences was a suggestion that the NHL drill a hole in the puck, because technically in proper French a "rondelle" has the sense of "washer," a round thing with a hole in it!

sin-bin – the penalty box. – Orr on *Ice*, p. 165.

slap shot – according to Schultz, a mid-1950s innovation in the game, "destructive to the game." "Until the arrival of Bernie Geoffrion, Andy Bathgate, and Bobby Hull, ... there were two basic shots employed by attackers – the forehand wrist shot and the backhand. In using the wrist shot, the offensive player cradled the puck at the end of his stick, then snapped his wrist and delivered the puck goalward. The backhand differed in that the puck was held on the stick with the stick on the side of the player's body opposite the side from which he would normally shoot. The rubber was fired goalward with a similar crack of the wrist. In neither case did the puck ever attain speeds of more than sixty miles per hour. In other words, the puck was always visible ... By allowing a player to wind up, golf-style, to swat the puck, "all of a sudden," says former NHL goalie Les Binkley, 'the puck became invisible.'" Schultz blames the slap shot for the invention of the goalie's "grotesque face mask to protect himself from a puck he never saw." Also known as SLAPPER, SLAP.

sleeper – see **floater,** in the sense "a player who..."

the slot – the area in front of the net between the two circles, on the ice surface. See also **crease.**

Smithonian save – type of save Islanders goalie Billy Smith was known for, named by Dick Irvin.

stand up goalie – goalie using traditional style, as distinguished from **flopper.**

Stanley Cup – "the trophy awarded annually to the NHL champion, winner of the best-of-seven Stanley Cup Championship Series... The oldest trophy competed for by professional athletes in North America, the Stanley Cup was donated by and named after Frederick Arthur, Lord Stanley of Preston, ... in 1893. – Tim Considine, *The Language of Sport.* First an amateur hockey trophy, it has been a professional prize since 1910, when the National Hockey Association took charge of it; at one point, the Quebec Bulldogs lost it to the Victoria (B.C.) Pacific Coast Hockey Association team, but refused to give up the cup itself (1913). (Considine, p. 214).

Star bag – the canvas bag with flap supplied to paperboys for delivery of the *Montreal Star,* a daily newspaper with wide circulation until its demise in the early 1980s, so often used for hockey equipment that it became a Montreal hockey term.

stick-boy – like "batboy" in baseball, the **rinkrat** who tends the equipment. Not to be confused with **stickman.**

stub – broken hockey stick, without a blade. "We still used them," Dryden, p. 57. See also **toothpicks.**

swamping the ice – instead of using the shift system, by which groups of five players each take turns, lasting from 30 seconds to two minutes, in play, in informal pickup games, there may be ten on a side, so that no one has to wait to play. Swamping the ice is thus not the same as **flooding the ice.**

in the tank – said of a team that is losing, and likely to lose. In the 1988 Stanley Cup playoffs, after the first game with the Boston Bruins, the Canadiens were "in the tank," though in this case it is only hindsight (or "Monday morning quarterbacking") that revealed it.

tiers-temps(Fr) – "period" in Europe. See also **vingt.**

tir(Fr) – "shot," **lancer.** It has been suggested that because "tir" does not have the sense of "throw" that "lancer" does, the cry "lance et compte!" should really be "tir et compte!"

toothpick – old wornout street hockey stick, without "tops on their blades," that is, the blade worn down, but still used, according to Dryden, p. 57. See also **stub.** The term "toothpick" also occurs in baseball, for the broken pieces of a bat.

top drawer, toy shelf, toy department – the top part of the goal. See **throws it upstairs,** and **up on the roof.** " 'During the exhibition season there are a lot of them ("goons") on every team,' Seaweed said, 'racing around and trying to make an impression. Goalies like us have to look out for them, because they're wild, and they'll put it up in the top drawer, shoot up on the roof a lot.'
"Up on the roof..."
"They'll throw the puck in high and bust you in the melon, like as not."
– George Plimpton, *Open Net*, New York: W.W. Norton, 1985, p. 35.

trailer – the last man to enter attacking zone and join the play, who because he is behind his teammates, may receive a drop or backward pass. Used in the same sense in basketball.

transversale(Fr) – "cross-ice," the European word for it. See **passe en diagonale.**

trio(Fr) – a line, Quebec usage. Literally: a three-some. In Europe it is "triplette." (Dallaire)

verglas(Fr) – "Scots word," according to Peter Gzowski (actually French for "glazed frost"), for "the hard surface of ice that is formed by precisely the right heaviness of rain falling on precisely the right bed of snow ... snow followed by rain, followed by a deep freeze," in Galt, Ontario, when he was "about ten." He describes the result: "After half an hour or so of playing our usual pick-up game, somebody accidentally shot the puck over the boards. Instead of burying itself, the puck slithered across the frozen surface, the *verglas.* Someone else went to chase it, and, miraculously, his skates held too. We followed the leader out into the park, skimming across the snow, firing infinitely long passes to each other. At the park's end, yelling excitedly to each other, we flung our sticks over the fence and headed for the open country. The snow held again, and off we went, soaring across roads and frozen lawns, like skiers who never had to climb their hills, and out, out into the country, by this time followed by every boy from our side of town who had skates – forty of us, fifty of us, gliding across farmer's fields, inventing new rules for our unending game, allowing for fences in the middle of a rush, or goals that might be half a mile apart. I didn't know if that had anything to do with hockey, I said to Brack, but I know I'd never been happier." – *The Game of Our Lives,* Toronto: McCIelland and Stewart, 1983, p. 106.

vingt(Fr) – period. Literally, a "twenty," for the number of minutes in a period of play. In Europe, it is **tierstemps.** (Dallaire)

Winnipeg curve – "a shape of hockey stick blade," according to Don McGillivray, Lingo column in *Southam News,* December 1989, reviewing Chris Thain's *Cold as a Bay Street Banker's Heart: The Ultimate Prairie Phrase Book* (1989). See also **banana blade.**

Zippers – "scars," according to Michael Farber, Montreal *Gazette.*

6. Tricks

A. SHOWING OFF.
Cool moves

airplane dive – "when a player, usually purposefully, dives forward onto her belly, the stick pushed ahead to deflect the opposing player's puck. Usually a defensive last-gap move. We practised them a lot – my favorite – the thing is to get up again within seconds." – from Abby (Feely) Curkeet.

Art Ross shot – in Boston, a shot "so slow you can read the writing on the puck as it comes by you."

backcheck – "working from behind the puck and player, trying to stop and seize the puck." – Orr on *Ice*, 86. "Skating back with your man."

banking it **in** – shooting the puck off the boards and into the opponent's zone. A term adapted from pool.

blind pass – passing without looking. Usually a **giveaway,** but it can be deceptive, a shot that looks like a giveaway but actually is accurately directed to a teammate.

bodychecking – "using only shoulder and hip, in two strides or less, trying to take the puck away from the puck-carrien" – *Orr on Ice*, p. 62.

Boston turn – "In Wisconsin, one of my coaches (from the LTW men's junior varsity) called a turn executed one foot ahead of the other (in a semicircle) a Boston turn. When done sharply, it's a way of stopping." – from Abby (Feely) Curkeet.

boulet(Fr) – "bullet," a very hard shot. "Hard/blazing/ blistering shot" – Dallaire. Part of the image cluster contained in **triggerman, sniper, gros canon, sharpshooter.**

breakout - to take the puck and advance up the ice. – "breakout of your own zone." This term is shared with basketball, where it also occurs as **breakaway.**

butterfly-type goalie – a stance originated by Glen Hall of Chicago in which the goalie's legs are wider apart, as distinguished from the classic "stand-up" goalie stance.

button-hooked – describes a particularly sharp turn around another player or the net. "Rocket buttonhooked around Armstrong."

cannonading - sportscaster Danny Gallivan's term for a hard slap-shot – "cannonading blast."

clear the puck – to get it out of one's own territory, the zone one is defending.

clear the slot – to shove an opposing player out of the area just in front of one's own goal.

close down the middle – spread out the offense by concentrating the defense on the area just in front of the **slot.** – from Ian Ferguson.

win in the **corners** – likely to be said of a team that is good at **mucking.** – from Ian Ferguson.

cradle the puck – the skill to move the puck expertly along. Not being able to do this results in **eggbeating** or **killing a snake.**

crisscross – according to Howard Liss, "an offensive play ... the wingmen cross the ice and change sides." *Hockey Talk for Beginners*, p. 23.

cut down the angle – said of the goalie, when he moves out from the crease in the direction of an expected shot, because on that side he leaves less space between himself and the goal post.

cycling – see ragging. – from Bill Fitsell.

dangle – "he can dangle" means "he stickhandles well," according to Michael Farber, Montreal *Gazette*.

deke – to outmaneuver an opponent, carrying the puck past him by feinting one way and then going the other. From "decoy." The word used for "deke" in the States during the thirties and forties was "feint." See Eddie Jeremiah, *Ice Hockey* (Barnes and Noble, 1942).

digger – "a hardskating man who sticks with the puck action until he assumes control." – Orr on *Ice*, p. 164.

dipsy-doodle – a term coined by Danny Gallivan to describe adroit skating with the puck. "Sundin's fluid dipsy-doodles soon had the tired Toronto defenders running in circles." – Quinn McIlhone, *Trade Rumors* , Toronto: McClelland and Steward, 1985, p. 38.

donner de la bande(Fr) – to check into the boards (Robinson & Smith).

win the **draw** – to capture the puck after a face-off.

draw a penalty – not to receive a penalty, but to act (or over-act) in such a way after a sharp check as to draw attention to the opposing player so that he receives a penalty. This term is also used in basketball. Drawing a penalty can often he accomplished by **taking a dive.**

dribbling – "keeping control and possession of the puck on the end of the stick with clever stickhandhng. " – Eddie Jeremiah, *Ice Hockey* (Barnes Sports Library, 1942). This term, shared with basketball, is peculiarly among hockey words a U.S. word and, according to Fem Flaman, six-time all-star defenseman for the Bruins and then hockey coach for Northeastern University in Boston, is still in use in high school and college hockey in the States. Jeremiah describes "dribbling" in detail: "While skating start your 'dribble' and then quickly place your stick blade in a position to receive your own 'dribble'before it gets away from you. When receiving your own 'dribble' have the blade in a quarter turned position so that it will form a good pocket and kill the force of any fast, hard dribble and at the same time prevent the puck from bouncing away This continuous 'dribbling' action, with its quarter turn stick action, is similar in movement to the honing of a straight edge razor on a strop." (p. 7) Jeremiah identifies three major "dribbles": the "lateral dribble," the "forward-backward dribble," and the "quick inside dribble." See also **stickhandling** and **tricoter.** The basketball meaning actually points to certain aspects of expert stickhandling that are not obvious to nonplayers: a good player will not skate along with the puck resting against the stick, because if he does, an opponent need not touch the puck to take it out of his control. A good hard blow to the stick, at any point, will make the puck fly off unless the stickhandler maintains intermittent contact, in some cases actually bounding the puck up and down as he moves down the ice. In this sense, *dribbling* is also used in soccer for a way of moving the ball that is more like the hockey meaning than the basketball.

dropping the gloves – customary way to announce during a hockey game that a fight is about to begin. Contrasts with "putting on the gloves," the familiar metaphorical expression in general usage for the same thing.

échappée(Fr) – breakaway. Literally, "escape." (Robinson & Smith)

empty net goal – a goal scored against a team which has "pulled the goalie."

end to end – see **coast to coast.**

face the guns – according to Gerry Cheevers, a goaltender's "purpose in life." – George Plimpton, *Open Net*, New York: WW Norton, 1985, p. 115. See also **triggerman.**

feathering the **puck** – a slow, perfectly timed pass. "How about Doug Harvey, better than Bobby Orr in so many ways, cradling the puck like a baby, feathering it to Maurice Richard, to Jean Beliveau ... " – Lawrence Martin, "Feel the Bruises, Hear the Roar," Toronto *Globe and Mail*, November, 1984. Why "feather" the puck? As Andy O'Brien describes it, it is so the "receiver could handle the puck for a quick shot instead of losing time in stopping, then nursing the puck into a comfortable position on the stick." – *Superstars: Hockey's Greatest Players*, p. 156.

finesse **players** – Players who have style and skill, who move the puck around well and score most of the goals. To be distinguished from **diggers** and **mucking out** (which see). "By the time the season opened, fate had boiled the roster down to a choice between him and Tomas Sundin, a brilliant playmaker directly from the Swedish nations, who was wary of going into the corners. Flynn got the nod. 'We have enough FINESSE PLAYERS on this team", Ranger coach Walcott muttered... "Gimme someone who goddamn well knows how to work." – Quinn McIlhone, *Trade Rumors*, Toronto: McClelland and Steward, 1985, p. 13. See **work.**

firedancing on ice – a way to describe brilliant play, attributed to Jim Coleman describing Howie Morenz. – Peter Gzowski, p. 124.

flip pass – in which the player "sends the puck a few inches above the ice so that the puck can 'hop over' an opponent's stick." Howard Liss, *Hockey Talk for Beginners.*

floater – "a player from the offensive team who sneaks into the center zone behind the attacking defensemen." – *Orr on Ice*, p. 164. See also **sleeper.** – a slow, drifting shot. See **knuckleball shot.**

follow-in – according to Howard Liss, "after a player takes a shot at the goal, it is good strategy for him to move quickly in toward the goal – to 'follow in' his shot – so that he is in position to capture a rebound or a clearing pass." - *Hockey Talk for Beginners.*

forecheck – "forcing the play by approaching puck and player with puck from in front, blocking his way with the body, especially with him in the corner."

frappé, frappée(Fr) – slap. As in "slap shot, slap pass," **lancer frappé, passe frappée.**

frappé court, frappée court(Fr) – snap, as in "snap shot," "snap pass," **lancer frappé court, passe frappée court.**

give and go – "a play in which the puckhandler passes the puck to a team-mate, then skates past one or more defenders to receive a return pass in the clear." Tim Considine, *The Language of Sport.*

give and take – According to Doug Beardsley, one of the goalie's tricks is to "give opposing forwards a glimpse at [**the shed** or **the five hole,** i.e. the space between the goalie's legs] before closing the pads.

and he glasses it for Goulet – "he shoots the puck high and at the side, causing it to ricochet off the glass into a spot where Goulet can get it and try to score" – from play by play description during the final games of the 1988 spring season.

gobbles up the puck – when it is loose in center ice, and one player skates through and grabs it, Danny Gallivan says "he gobbles up the puck."

handcuffed – "the goalie was handcuffed on the play." A shot right at the goalie's face, or a high shot which he must reach up for after having gone down, or a **knuckleball shot** (which see) – a shot exceptionally difficult to block.

hang them on the glass – said of Brad Park (See **Brad**): "a beautiful brute, he loves to hang 'em on the glass." – Dana Mozley, *New York Daily News*, quoted in Andy O'Brien, *Superstars: Hockey's Greatest Players*, p. 132.

headman the puck – pass the puck up and just ahead of the player receiving the pass, the farthest up the ice.

he shoots, he scores! – verbal trademark of the hockey live coverage by Foster Hewitt, first used in 1933, according to a CBC obituary notice on April 22, 1985.

hipcheck – "you let your man come to you and then get your hip into him." – *Orr on Ice*, p. 68. The action has been compared to slam-dancing.

in there – "he was *in there*" means he made an effective move, almost scored, but it is not used when the move results in a goal, unless occasionally for an assist.

jamming the **puck** – tying it up against the boards, stopping play so that a faceoff is necessary.

Jesus saves but Orr scores on the rebounds – Montreal wall graffiti. "Orr" is sometimes replaced in this well-known saying by Esposito or Lafleur ... The most elaborate version has it: *Jesus saves but Orr picks up the rebound and scores!*

Jesus saves but Espo scores on the rebounds another occurrence of the phrase, this time applied to Phil Esposito.

journeyman player – in baseball, a steady, dependable player; in hockey, more derogatory, to say that a player lacks flash, brilliance, but makes up for it with hard work.

juke – to fake or shift an opponent, as in "He juked him out of his jockstrap!"

the knuckleball shot – a slow, perfectly timed shot which, as the puck seems to float, edge over edge, imitates the twisting, confusingly slowing "knuckleball pitch" of baseball.

labelled drive – a drive which is obvious, planned, and coordinated toward the goal, with the aim of scoring. According to Doug Beardsley, stopping one is the greatest satisfaction a goalie can have. – *Country* On *Ice.*

load the rubber on – to score goals against. "Beliveau reached 200 goals with a four-goal splurge... against one of the game's all-time goaling greats, Terry Sawchuk... He hadn't really intended to load the rubber on Terry" since the Canadiens held an 8-2 lead by the early third period, but "I realized I had only one goal to go for my 200th and maybe I'd go five or six games without it unless I got it tonight. I dreaded the pressure that would mean, so ... " – Andy O'Brien, *Superstars*, p. 72.

making the shift – moving the puck expertly from one side to the other to fool a defenceman, a trick in superb stickhandling. See STICKDEKING.

motoring – showing one's great effort in speed and heart. "He's really motoring out there."

museler l'adversaire(Fr) – to "box in an opponent," to hold onto the puck expertly, successfully, incontestably. (Dallaire) The French phrase is different in imagery from the English "box" – it is "to muzzle," "to gag," etc.

one-time it – The offensive player takes his backswing while the puck is on the way to him and tries to time his swing with the arrival of the puck. Immediately shooting on goal, he "one-times it!"

ouvrir la machine(Fr) – to "blast off", attack furiously, attack at full speed." (Dallaire) The French imagery is contained in the English expression describing Canadiens' style of play: **firewagon hockey.**

passout – "a pass by an attacking player from behind an opponent's goal to a teammate who is in front of the goal." – Howard Liss, *Hockey Talk for Beginners*.

peeling the banana – to come in from a breakaway and fake to one side or another of the goalie, to make him open his legs, then shoot it between them.

penalty shot – awarded after an offensive player, with no defender between him and the goal, is checked illegally, hauled down, etc. The puck is placed at the centre ice faceoff spot. The player has a free try at the opposing goalie, with no defenders on the ice.

pick the corner – to make a well-aimed scoring shot which just goes in the corner of the net. – from Ian Ferguson.

pinching – moving in on the winger, limiting his freedom of movement and reducing his chances of getting a shot at the net. Also, when on offense, a defenseman can "pinch in" and thus get a good scoring opportunity, in the power-play.

poke check – "With the stick close to the body and extended at full length, 'poking' the puck off the opponent's stick." – *Orr on Ice*, p. 69. A French word for "poke-check" is "crochet." See also Robinson and Smith, *Practical Handbook of Quebec and Acadian French* (Anansi, 1984), p. 194.

powdered – a shot which is hit hard. It literally shaves off bits of ice, a little cloud, as stick meets puck and smokes the ice. Compare **smoking section, smoker.**

the puck had eyes – said of an uncannily accurate shot.

puck sense – uncanny ability to know where the puck is going to go. – Stan Fischler, *Bobby Orr and the Big Bad Bruins*, p. 73. Best pro examples are Orr and Gretzky.

pylon skater – a fast, artful skater, a player who can do "slalom" on skates. – from Ian Ferguson.

quarterback – metaphorical use of this word imported from football: "he's a real quarterback," means he sees everything, he is a playmaker.

ragging the puck – "super stickhandling as a player keeps ownership of the puck." - *Orr on Ice*, p. 165. Can also be used for play in which the stickhandling is not really intended to move the puck toward the goal but rather to keep it moving so as to keep possession and control. The word echoes RAGGER, a term from basketball for a player who keeps the ball selfishly, who does not pass to teammates, and RAG THE BALL, a basketball term for play by several teammates designed to keep the ball away from the other team, to use up time on the clock to protect a lead.

Russian weave – a name for the style of play which startled the West when Russian hockey became better known here, characterized by a complex alternation of roles by the players on the ice, defensive players taking the offense, offensive players taking the defense, in a fluid and efficient way. – from Abby (Feely) Curkeet.

Sawchuk – "shutout," according to Michael Farber, Montreal *Gazette*.

screen shot – shot made from behind a screen made by one or more players. *Orr on Ice*, p. 165, calls it a "screened shot" and "screened goal" is a term used. See Schultz, pp. 204-5: "By the late 1960s coaches organized their strategy so that the vision of the goalie was blocked altogether. It now became fashionable for attackers to congregate in front of the net with the express purpose of blocking the netminder's view. Some goaltenders accepted the condition without protest, but others, especially Billy Smith of the New York Islanders, responded by chopping at the legs of any enemy who camped near his crease. 'I'm not asking for much,' said Smith, 'just a chance to see the puck. And if they won't let me, I'll make damn sure they pay the price with their legs.' " Peter Chipman, of Winnipeg, who in the 1950s played for Navy teams in international competition ashore, remembers that in Japan, because of the cultural emphasis on never defeating an opponent in a way that caused him to lose face, the

Japanese players would not shoot screen shots. The goalie had to be able to see the puck.

seeing-eye dribbler – a slow shot that uncannily finds the goal open. "The first [goal] was a 'seeing-eye' dribbler off the stick of defenceman Scot Kleinendorst which took most of the period's first fifteen seconds to skitter through a forest of skates and sticks and into the corner past a thoroughly screened Roy." (Goyens and Turowetz 1986:377-8).

sharpshooter – goal scorer. Schultz, p. 131: "Shero .. had no intention of having me change my style. He had made that clear to me when he said I wasn't a sharpshooter or a playmaker... Even if I wanted to go straight, I said to myself, I couldn't."

shorthanded – playing with fewer than six on a side, usually because one or more is in the penalty box. A SHORTHANDED GOAL is a particular triumph.

shot blocker – defenseman like Bob Goldham of the Red Wings who'd slide across the ice to block a shot with his body, **shoots a good stick** – accurate dependable goal scorer. Orr, in Fischler, p. 207, lists as an example Derek Sanderson.

showboater – a flashy, confident player, like Tiger Williams, who does not hide his pleasure when he scores a goal, doing stunts like pirouetting with his stick between his legs, as if it were a very large penis, etc.

shy – "You go near him in the corner and you'll see he's not shy." (He is not afraid to use his stick on you, not just on the puck). See also PUCK-SHY.

skater – a refined, skillful player, the opposite of an **enforcer**. Someone who always rushes the **play**, is always on top of the puck, always comes back in the play.

smoker – a hard slapshot from the point. See **smoking section, no smoking section.**

he's been **snakebitten** tonight – he's jinxed, playing well but can't seem to score. "He was robbed," or "the goalie's got a horseshoe up his ass" are two other **ways** to say the same thing.

snapshot – "a shot made by a quick action of the wrist, directing the puck suddenly and accurately at the goal." - *Dictionary of Canadianisms.* Distinguished from **slapshot.**

he's got **soft hands with the puck** – how Pat Burns, Hull Olympiques coach, describes the good stickhandling of Joe Foglietta. Also a term used in basketball for a player with exceptional skill at ballhandling.

specialist – according to Dryden, (p. 30), Steve Shutt, a specialist, not a **garbageman,** "lurks about in the weeds, away from the play, unnoticed in a game that centers around his linemate Lafleur. Then as the puck enters an opponent's zone, he accelerates to the net like a dragster, with quick, chopping strides, to sweep in a goalmouth pass, to deflect a shot in some improbable way, to snap a rebound to a top corner. It is a style he learned as a boy in a small backyard rink his father built. Crowded with neighbourhood kids, there was little room to skate and only time for short, quick shots that gave no second chance." A specialist is any player who uses a certain skill to its utmost, makes up for his shortcomings by fulfilling a certain role on the ice, in which he specializes. In this sense, even an enforcer like Schultz is a specialist of sorts.

a real **spinnerama** – Danny Gallivan's term for a brilliant deceptive shot made while spinning around or pivoting.

split the defense – to go through the middle with the puck. – from Ian Ferguson.

spot pass – "passing to a spot on the ice instead of a player" – *Orr on Ice*, p. 164.

stick-deking – to hold the puck on one side of the stick, teasing the defenceman, than when he goes for it, you pull it to the other side and you're gone!" Also called **making the shift.**

stickhandling – skill at maneuvering the puck with the stick. See also **dribbling.** The Quebec term for this skill is "tricoter," "knitting." It is said of Makarov, formerly of the Soviets and later with Calgary, that he can "**stickhandle in a phone booth.**"

stretch passes – passes made up the middle. – from Bill Fitsell.

sweepcheck – "as he approaches, wait until you can reach him with your extended stick. Put the stick flat on the ice. Use it like a broom and sweep the puck away." – *Orr on Ice*, p. 74.

taking a dive – falling dramatically so as to suggest that an opponent's check was brutal and illegal, bringing down a penalty upon him. See also **draw a penalty.** A term used in the same sense in football.

throws it upstairs – shoots the puck into the top corner of the net. Known also as the **top shelf,** the **top drawer,** and the **toy department.** This term is also used in baseball, for the pitch known better as the **bean ball,** the **brushback,** or the memorable **got into his kitchen,** when the pitcher deliberately throws the ball at the batter's head. See also **up on the roof.**

thundering shot – a Danny Gallivanism for a hard, non-scoring shot which hits the boards hard, making a booming, echoing noise. Related to **cannonading.** pointed out by Ian Ferguson.

tied him up – stopped his progress and interfered with his exclusive possession of the puck by trapping him or the puck against the boards, or just getting in his way, tying him up in any way possible, with a stick between the legs and one arm draped over his shoulder, and so forth. Used also in baseball for a good pitch, just inside but over the plate and therefore in the strike zone in an area in which a batter, standing too close, cannot get a good swing and therefore cannot hit it anywhere but foul.

tir percutant, tir violent(Fr) – hard, blazing, blistering shot.

top gun – a player who scores many goals a season, like 50 plus. "One of them [two excellent goalies] perhaps could go [be traded] for a top gun." – Francis Rosa, "Trader Phil's dealings get Rangers wheeling," Boston Globe (November 10, 1988), discussing Phil Esposito's options in view of the fact that, as New York Ranger general manager, he has a team with many strengths, but "we just don't have a 50-goal scorer."

tour de chapeau, truc du chapeau (Fr)- "hat trick," a player's scoring three goals in one game. A term from cricket. -

transversale(Fr) – "cross-ice," the European word for it. See **passe en diagonale.**

tricoter(Fr) – stickhandling, or in the United States, "dribbling," "keeping control and possession of the puck on the end of the stick with clever stickhandling." Eddie Jeremiah, *Ice Hockey* (Barnes Sports Library, 1942). Most curiously, The European word for "tricoter, tricotage"(knitting) according to Dallaire, is **dribbler, dribblage.**

triggerman – a hot scorer. See also **sniper** and **face the guns.**

wheeling – playing well. "He's really wheeling in his own zone.

he's got good **wood to it** – to describe a hard shot. Also a baseball term. To GET GOOD WOOD ON IT is to make solid contact between stick and puck. The correct spot, for good wood, is between the heel and the toe of the stick, just forward of the heel.

wraparound – a shot made from beside the goal by poking the puck around the pole and tucking it in.

B. DIRTY TRICKS

ash surgery – violent attack on the opponent's body with the stick – "Billy Couture (often known as Coutu) a former Canadien with a penchant for ash surgery, who as a Boston Bruin in 1927 would he banned for life from hockey for attacking a referee." – Goyens and Turowetz 1986:41.

Bad Man – according to Howard Liss, "any hockey player who picks fights, checks much harder than necessary or joins a fight between two other players." *Hockey Talk for Beginners*, New York: Julian Messner, 1973.

blindsided – what happens when a player is hit by a vicious check from behind. A term also used in football.

to **give** someone a **Brad** – to give someone a sharp hip**check,** named for Brad Park, for eight seasons a New York Ranger, then after 1976 a Boston Bruin, a specialist in the hip-check.

Broadstreet shuffle – the **dance** so commonly engaged in on the ice, the fighting which was the trademark of the Philadelphia Flyers in the 1970s, the Broadstreet Bullies.

butt ending – making the opposing player impale himself on one's stick, or jabbing him with the butt end of one's stick, a dirty trick. Known in Quebec as "donner six pouces," ("give six inches"), and there and elsewhere as "to give him six inches of good wood."

chippy – dirty, rough. "He's a real chippy player." "The funny thing is that when people talk about Clarke the cute little word 'chippy' keeps popping up. How about 'dirty'?" – Dave Schultz, *The Hammer*, p. 119.

coldcocked – hit from behind. – from Stephen Scriver, *The All-Star Poet*, p. 66. See also **blindsided.**

crackback check – a really hard check against the boards, perhaps a retaliation blow.

crochet (Fr) – poke check – "With the stick close to the body and extended at full length, 'poking' the puck off the opponent's stick." – *Orr on Ice*, p. 69. Like "tricoter," the word comes from women's crafts ...

dance – fight. "Once in a while we have a dance, even with a black eye." – *Orr* on Ice, **p.** 150. "It takes two to tango." – Schultz, 1943. Also called "the waltz."

donner de la bande (Fr)- to check into the boards (Robinson & Smith).

donner un six pouces (Fr)- butt ending, making the opposing player impale himself on one's stick, or jabbing him with the butt end of one's stick, a dirty trick. Literally, to "give six inches" or more fully "to give him six inches of good wood."

putting on the **foil** – applying tinfoil layers under the gloves to increase the impact of punches in fights, a practice recorded in Nancy Dowd's script for the movie Slap Shot. A **goon** tactic.

glove-rubbed – description of a retaliatory move by Rocket Richard in a December 28, 1944, game with Toronto: "Rocket peevishly glove-rubbed Max Bentley's face without referee Red Storey noticing. Bob Armstrong lost his cool, deserted his post in front of Henry and moved to cut off the outlaw." – Andy O'Brien, *Superstars: Hockey's Greatest Players*, p. 33.

go – fight. "He's been known to GO." See also **dance.**

hacker – see entry under "Who."

harponnage(Fr) – "poke checking." The term literally means "harpooning."

hatchetman – player valued for his aggressive, intimidating, fighting style of play rather than his skill. One who is guided by Conn Smythe's "If you can't beat them in the alley, you can't beat them on the ice." Schultz, p. 195.

headhunters – high, wide slapshots or players with really high, wide slapshots.

highsticking – illegal tactic, hitting an opposing player with the stick held above shoulder level, or, for that matter, having the stick up that high at all.

hook – hold the opposing player back (illegally) with one's stick. Memorialized in Nancy Dowd's script for the movie Slap Shot in the figure of Dr. Hook, a particularly vicious player skilled with the stick-as-hook.

Hudson Bay Rules – Heard at a Leafs' intersquad scrimmage: "It's Hudson Bay Rules, anything goes." – from Doug Gilmour.

jeter les gants(Fr) – to fight, to "drop the gloves" ("se battre") (Dallaire). Literally "to *throw* the gloves!" The French expression is much more colourful and dramatic (and true to the event) than the English, for as the **dance** starts, the **échauffourée**, the gloves are thrown, not just "laisser tomber," "let fall," or "dropped!"

laying on the lumber – a Danny Gallivan expression for **cross-check**ing. they're going to be **laying the body on** – a prediction of sharp checking and aggressive physical confrontation, rather than skilled or brilliant play.

lights-out maneuver – a term for pulling the opponent's sweater over his head, not for knocking him unconscious.

lumber – the stick, especially when it is used for other than stick-handling and shooting. "He got the lumber in his teeth." This term has affinities with baseball lingo; for their powerful hitting, the Pittsburgh Pirates in their best days were known as the "Lumber Company."

mucking it **up** – "protecting one's rights, not letting anyone get advantage of you, fighting... " – "Seaweed," a rookie goalie for the Bruins, as quoted by George Plimpton, *Open Net*, New York: WW Norton, 1985, p. 28.

a mugging – a particularly severe loss in the Boston Beanpot tournament.

Northland sandwich – "Someone called out, 'Hey, Georgie, give them the Northland sandwich!' 'What's the Northland sandwich?' 'That's the brand name on your stick, for Chrissake... stick it in their teeth is what I'm saying.'" – George Plimpton, *Open Net*, (New York: Norton, 1985).

pitchfork – to attempt to spear an opposing player with the stick, by thrusting it toward him at waist-level and swinging it upward. An illegal act. "And Green tries to pitchfork him!"

poke check – "With the stick close to the body and extended at full length, 'poking' the puck off the opponent's stick." – *Orr on Ice*, p. 69. A French word for "poke-check" is "crochet." See also Robinson and Smith, *Practical Handbook of Quebec and Acadian* French (Anansi, 1984), p. 194.

put him in the third row or **put him in the stand** - hit him hard. "You really put him in the third row with that check! But he asked for it."

ringing the berries – hitting the goalie with a hard shot between the legs. The puck hits a special hard molded plastic protective cup, worn in addition to the athletic supporter, which "gives off a high bong," a sound which is known as "ringing the berries," according to George Plimpton, *Open Net*, New York: WW. Norton, 1985, p. 42.

to give him a **shot** with one's stick – to attack another player with the stick. The image owes as much to the set of connotations of, and the original speech community from which **sniper** and **triggerman** come as to the associations with "taking a shot on goal." "I gave him a shot with my stick and broke his ankle" – Elkan Levitan, a goalie in the Canadiens' organization in the 1930s, describing what he did to one player when he got "fed up with guys skating through the crease and giving him the elbow." – from Jack Todd's Column, Montreal Gazette, January 26, 1990. Another use of the word in hockey, illustrated in the same interview, is a form of the more conventional meaning, "to have a chance," "to have an opportunity": "I had a shot at making it with the old Montreal Royals, but they didn't like my attitude."

slashing – chopping at the opponent with the stick. See also **two hander.**

spear – to poke or stab an opponent with the end of the stick. Illegal tactic of a **headhunter.**

tell him it's his birthday – sarcastic way of saying, "in retaliation, attack him!" (with a sharp check, a hook, a slash, an elbow, etc.)

twohander – a swing of the stick using both hands, not necessarily for a shot on goal. "The two-hander was one of Bobby (Clarke's) standard weapons. It often was employed by him – and by many other Flyers – after the enemy had scored, as an act of retribution In a game we played against the Canadiens in February 1974, Murray Wilson of Montreal had just scored a goal and Clarke was right behind him. 'After I put the puck in the net,' Wilson said later, 'Clarke whacked me a good two-hander on the left arm.'" – Schultz, p. 120.

ventilated – see **air conditioned.**

woodwork – used on CBC October 28, 1985, to describe a crosscheck in which Stasny hit an opponent high with the stick.

7.
Wrong moves

barely got his crest on it – "squandering a shot by shooting fight at the goalie," from M. Farber, Montreal *Gazette*. See **way to break in his pads.**

cement hands – slow or inaccurate shooter (Don Cherry, May 12, 1985).

cherrypicker – another term for a guy who gets cheap goals, who waits at the center line for an easy shot when the puck's in his zone. See also **nethanger. A term** also used in basketball for the same sort of **player.**

coughing up the puck – losing the puck to an opposing player.

crackback check – a really hard cheek against the **boards, perhaps a** retaliation blow.

dégagement illegal, dégagement refusé (Robinson & Smith), **dégagement irrégulier (Fr)** (Dallaire) – icing (the puck).

échauffourée (Fr)- "bagarre," "fight, fisticuffs." Literally: an event heated in the oven. Compare the English: "a dance."

fan – to fan on the shot is to attempt a slap shot, swinging but missing the puck. "He fanned on it" Danny Gallivan. A term also used, of course, in baseball.

flip-flop – double **turnover** via missed passes, errors.

flopper – "a goaltender who hits the ice too much trying to make saves' " - *Orr on Ice*, p. 164. The goalie's dropping to the ice is sometimes called the "Fosbury flop," from the high jump style of a world record high jumper, Dick Fosbury, in the early'70s, who went over the crossbar head first and backwards, making for a high jump but an awkward landing. According to Tim Considine, the NHL first allowed a goalie to dive or flop without a two-dollar fine around 1918. (*The Language of sport*, p. 215.

giveaway – a shot, pass, or move that carelessly gives the puck away to the other team.

gloved ahead – a procedural infraction that occurs when a player intercepts the puck with his or her glove and then instead of dropping it directly beside or behind, to move it with the stick, tosses it out ahead toward the goal. There's no penalty, but the whistle stops play and a face-off occurs.

high on the stick side – according to Doug Beardsley, "a major weakness for young goalies," a place where goals get scored on them. – *Country on Ice*.

hit the pipe – almost score by making the puck strike the metal goalpost and rebound. See **between the pipes**.

hog – player who holds the puck too long and usually ends up "coughing it up" (which see) in deep or throwing fellow players offside.

hoisting – term used in some places in central and western Canada, and in Boston at times, for what is otherwise known as "lifting," i.e. hitting the puck so that it rises, making it more dangerous to plate glass windows near an outdoor rink, or goalies without equipment. "No Lifting" appears on Boston rinks; "no hoisting!"

icing – "icing is called when a player on a team equal or superior in strength shoots, bats, or deflects the puck from his own half of the ice, beyond the goal line of the opposing team." – *Orr on Ice*, p. 156. "Play is stopped and the puck faced-off at the end face-off spot of the offending team." This commonly used term describes a complex situation: "an infraction in which a player shoots or directs the puck from behind the center red line (or from the defensive zone in amateur play) across the opposing team's goal line, where it is then touched first by an opposing player other than the goaltender. Icing is not called if the puck is played (or, in the judgment of the officials, could be played) by an opposing player before it crosses the goal line, if it is first touched by the defending goaltender, if it is played first by a teammate (who is not offside) of the player who directed or shot the puck into the zone, if it is driven into the zone directly from a faceoff, if the team sending the puck into the zone is playing shorthanded, or if the puck enters the goal for a score. When icing is called, play is resumed with a faceoff in the offending team's defensive zone." – Tim Considine, *The Language of Sport*.

jambette (Fr)- Quebec regionalism, in "donner une jambette," for "to trip," "accrocher," literally meaning to "give the little leg," or adapted from house construction, "to cross-brace," a jocular and humorous way to say it. (Dallaire)

no smoking section – also called the SLOT, an area immediately in front of the net where a "flick" or "SNAP" shot (which see) is more effective than a slap shot. In no-equipment street hockey, a slapshot in this area is dangerous to the goalie, a rule against them is strictly observed, and the zone usually extends out twenty to thirty feet from the net. See also **smoking section, smoker.**

palming the puck – stopping the puck with the glove, by anyone but the goalie, an illegal way to **freeze the puck.**

réchauffer le banc(Fr) – to be benched, literally to "warm up the bench." A jocular expression like the English "to ride the pines." (Robinson & Smith)

rockhead move – a really stupid move.

turnover – change in control of the puck, when one team loses it to the other. Dryden, p. 223. A term also used in football and basketball.

way to break in his pads! – "squandering a good scoring chance by shooting directly at the goalie," spoken sarcastically, according to Michael Farber, Montreal *Gazette*.

8. Ouch! -
INJURIES

air conditioned – "bloodied up": "Before he hit the ice Doug hit him with his stick and he was ventilated, I think, for about fifteen stitches, all air-conditioned for the summer, and when the blood started to flow it sort of stopped things but they never stopped throwing ... " – Red Storey, describing an incident in a game in Chicago, the sixth game of the 1959 Stanley Cup **series,** between Chicago and Montreal. From Sandy Jenkins' *Yellow Sunday*.

ash surgery – see entry under "Dirty Tricks."

he's got a **bad wheel** – he's not skating well, perhaps due to a knee injury. See also **wheeling.**

claquage, contracture (Fr)- "charley horse," literally, a "snap," a "clap," a "bang," a "contraction."

crackback check – see entry under "Dirty Tricks."

heavy shot – a shot so hard goalies say it hurts when it hits them, probably because it hits them flat on, not on the edge. – from Ian Ferguson.

jumble your Chiclets – offhand way of brushing off a direct hit to the mouth: "Aww, that one just jumbled my Chiclets!"

on the **limp** – in a cast or otherwise injured: "If Orr and I could collect all that stuff (awards) while on the limp, Sinden's liable to break everybody's knees in training camp next September." – Phil Esposito, quoted in Andy O'Brien, *Superstars*, p. 29.

pitchfork – see entry under "Dirty Tricks."

playing his **way** back into **shape** – according to Doug Beardsley, management's explanation of the habit of opposition and teammates of "testing [a goalie's] nerve by cranking a few slapshots at eye level" after he has been injured by a shot to the head. It's to see if he's **puck-shy.** Beardsley comments, "the players know the real reason." -*Country on Ice.*

ventilated – see **air conditioned.**

zippers – see entry under "What is that."

9. How to...
ADVICE, RULES, AND LORE

American rules – no center red line in use. Speeds up the game and cuts down on two-line passes and offsides. Used a lot in intramural college games and senior leagues. – from Leslie Bairstow.

the bigger you are, the harder they fall – hockey law of the jungle. – Schultz, p. 67,

bodychecking – "using only shoulder and hip, in two strides or less, trying to take the puck away **from** the puck-earrien" – *Orr on Ice*, p. 62.

brothers together **play better** – hockey maxim, prompted by the success of such brother teaimates as the Richards (Maurice, Henry, of the Canadiens), the Stasnys (Peter, Anton, Marian, of the Nordiques), etc.

follow-in – according to Howard Liss, "after a player takes a shot at the goal, it is good strategy for him to move quickly in toward the goal – to 'follow in' his shot – so that he is in position to capture a rebound or a clearing pass." - *Hockey Talk for Beginners*.

forecheck, backcheck, paycheck! – coach's exhortation in pro hockey to encourage defensive play and remind players of how much they get paid to make their presence felt out on the ice. From Ken Dryden's *The Game*, p. 179.

forecheck in tandem! – hard-driving coach's yell to young players, probably during a drill, in municipal league hockey, in Ken Dryden's Home Game, CBC-TV February 11, 1990. Means "synchronize your forechecking, do it together, keeping each other eye on the other forward as well as the puck!"

homers – a team of players who play well on home ice. Ken Dryden, reporting the pro coach's exhortations to his players, lists "home reasons" to play hard, like 'let's be homers, guys,' and also 'road reasons' – "Let's not be homers, guys." – p. 179. This term is also sometimes applied to announcers prejudiced in favour of the home team.

icing – see entry under "wrong moves"

Jesus saves but Orr scores on the rebounds – see entry under "Tricks."

Jesus saves but Espo scores on the rebounds see entry under "Tricks."

lance et compte(Fr) - "shoot and score," derived from announcer Foster Hewitt's ritual exclamation "He shoots! He scores!" despite such attempts to make it "et c'est le but!" or et il marque!" as that by Dallaire and others. One (anglophone) player told me that he had heard that French announcers for the Canadiens had been forbidden by the Molsons, owners of the team, to use the expression because it may be easily mis-heard as "lance cinquante" – "shoot for a 50," thus providing a bit of free advertising for the competitor beer brewing company Labatt. He claimed that they always say "Lance et but!," but then he also said that he didn't know any French hockey phrases because he watches the game on the French channel on TV when it isn't televised in English but tums the sound off and listens to the play-by-play on the English radio station.

In Europe, according to Dallaire, it is "shoot et goal!"

no Lifting! – a Boston rule which prohibits shots which bring the puck higher than one's waist.

Offense sells tickets. Defense wins championships. – ancient sports maxim.

play the man – advice from Bobby Orr: "To defend against the deke, keep your eyes glued steadily on your opponent's chest." – *Orr on Ice*, p. 97. "Midway through the 1968-69 season, Derek (Sanderson) had developed a theory about the Canadiens – 'If you play the man, they won't get started.' " (Fischler, *Bobby* Orr *and the Big, Bad Bruins*, p. 207). Instead of following the puck, which with a good stickhandler will make you dizzy, watch the opponent's body and "ride him off the puck;" don't let him go by you."

the puck had eyes – said of an uncannily accurate shot.

put him in the third row or **put him in the stands** – see entry under "Dirty Tricks."

shaivu! or **shaibu!** – Russian shout of encouragement, meaning literally, "the puck."

the Shave – a hockey rookie initiation ritual, described by Schultz, p. 127: "in which a player was placed on a table and literally shaved, pubic hair and all – top to bottom." It is probably not true that this practice originated in Catholic Quebec in imitation of a practice common during the novitiate stage of the training of monks and nuns.

stick 'im! – yelled, to encourage someone to jab an opponent with his stick, to "butt-end him: or "give him six inches of good wood."

you can teach them **how to fight,** you can't teach them how to shoot and score – hockey maxim. Glen Sather, coach of the Edmonton Oilers, has been credited with this saying.

use the body – an injunction to aggressive play. "'Use the body' was a theme that was repeated so often it became permanently etched in my brain." – Dave Schultz, *Confessions of Hockey Enforcer,* p. 68.

win or tie – key phrase in a Montreal hockey coaches' rule of thumb: "In this town, as the joke goes, the media and the fans are with you win or tie, but don't tie too often." Goyens and Turowetz 1986:379, quoting Jean Perron.

10. Have another donut!

INSULTS

after the skates go **blunt** – see entry under "When."

clutch and grab – a style of play characterized by close checking, usually played by a team of "grinders." – from Jonathan Weissman.

clutch and slash – derogatory term for the newer style of play, by Sandy Jenkins, who remembers more fondly the days "when the shoulder or hip check rather than the clutch and slash stopped the winger as he swept gracefully to the net." - *Yellow Sunday* , p. 6.

Detroit Dead Things, Dead Wings, Dead Things derogatory names for the Detroit Red Wings.

doughnut – a shutout, score of 0 for one team. "Ready for another doughnut?" – Paul Quarrington, Logan in *Overtinw* (Doubleday, 1990).

have another **donut you fat pig!** – insult yelled by Jim Schonefeld, coach of the New Jersey Devils, at Ron Koharski, referee, in the Stanley Cup Playoffs of 1988, during the game (May 6) with the Bruins after which Schonefeld was suspended for one game. The suspension was probably for more than the words, but they didn't hurt. The incident soon was known as "The Great Donut Caper." –

from Jeff Knight. For a detailed account of this event and more, on violence in professional hockey, see Sandy Jenkins' *Yellow Sunday.*

douche bags – "In one game [in which men and women were playing] a particularly obnoxious male opponent berated men and women alike on our team, referring to us all as "douche bags" – not a hockey term per se, but I finally hip checked him hard into the boards." from Abby (Feely) Curkeet.

Dr. Hook – nickname of Bobby Schmautz, Boston Bruin, late 1970s.

Elmer – see entry under "Hockey Talking."

Fast legs, slow fist – a line used to describe a player with speed and skill who has not yet learned to fight, or to want to fight. - *Youngblood*, a U.S. movie about hockey, 1985.

the puck doesn't **find you the way it used to** – Ken Dryden's way of describing a player's unhappy and gradual discovery that he is competing out of his depth, when he thought he was "on the **pro course.**" In Home Game, CBC-TV February 11, 1990.

finesse players – may be used insultingly. See entry under "Tricks – a. Showing Off."

garbage man – player who scores garbage goals. According to Ken Dryden, Steve Shutt "is often disparaged as a'garbage man.'But he is not. Rather, he is what laughingly he says he is, a 'specialist.' " See **specialist.** Another term for "garbage man" is "garbage collector," and Phil Esposito is given as an example, for his sixty or more goals in one season.

on the **golf course,** or ready for the **golf course** – said of a team that is ending the season with no hope of making the playoffs.

golf shot – somewhat contemptuous term for a windup and swing that doesn't score.

goon coach – after the 1984 playoff series in which Quebec eliminated the Buffalo Sabres, Buffalo coach Scotty Bowman called Quebec Nordiques coach Michel Bergeron a "goon coach" for his use of enforcer Jimmy Mann *(Globe and* Mail, October 26, 1985, page D3).

goons – a team which relies more on its players' size, strength, and vicious, dirty techniques. Such a team may be recognized by the odd Flyers sweater, worn by a player whose heroes are the Philadelphia Flyers in the late seventies, known as the **Broadstreet bullies** (which see). Also known as **ice thugs** (see George Plimpton, *Open Net*, New York: WW Norton, 1985, p. 95).

the **Great Donut Caper** – see **Donutgate** and **Yellow Sunday.**

hacker – see entry under "Dirty Tricks."

the Hammer – nickname of Dave Schultz, enforcer of the **Broadstreet bullies.**

ice thugs – another term for GOONS (which see).

Loose Leafs – derogatory nickname of Toronto Maple Leafs, overheard in Montreal.

Maple Laffs, Maple Loafs – derogatory nicknames for the Toronto Maple Leafs.

plumbers – derogatory term for unexceptional players. Dick Irvin, during April 23, 1986 game between Montreal and Hartford: "the goalscorers get those kind of goals and the plumbers don't."

pylon – a player who is so bad a skater and so slow that good players have to skate around him, as if he were the obstacle in a slalom or practice driving course. – from Chris Coyle.

rabbit ears – thin-skinned players or officials.

scheiss-eie – "shitty egg," in German: a curse directed at the puck after a semi-pro player in West Germany wound up, took a "golf shot," and missed. – Dana Johnson.

scrubs – derogatory term for hockey players. "He thinks we're a bunch of scrubs. He'd rather be playing with Daniel Mac." – from Scott Young's *Scrubs on Skates..* The term probably comes from the term for players who are rejected from a team's roster, or "scrubbed" from the chalkboard list.

he's got no **seeds** – an insult, a put-down, worse than being called "cement-head," probably derived from a slang term for the head – the "melon."

sieve – derogatory term for poor defensive play. Especially used a lot around Madison, Wisconsin. "Whenever the opposing goalie allows a puck through his net, the uproarous Wisconsin fans, 8000 of them, rise in unison, point at the poor sap, and yell 'sieve, sieve, sieve,' implying of course that he is one where pucks apply." – from Abby (Feely) Curkeet.

Three Blind Mice – one tune forbidden to be played in the Forum, the Canadiens' arena in Montréal, because its being played by the organist in obvious reference to the referees sparked the famous Rocket Richard riot during the Stanley Cup playoffs in the mid1950s.

we're gonna **train you for the front office** – in Nancy Dowd's script for the movie Slap Shot, a sarcastic way of telling a player that he may soon be retired from active play.

he must have **tripped over the blue line** – insulting jocular comment when someone pulls a **Zamboni** (which see) with no other players around.

windup skater – a player who is slow at starting and stopping. Paul Coffey, Edmonton Oilers defenceman, says "I never tried to pattem myself after Orr because that would have been stupid. I think he had better moves than me in tight. Stopping and starting, he had quicker moves. I'm a windup skater." – William Houston, in *The Globe and Mail*, October 10, 1985.

woodchopper – enforcer, hatchetman, one who uses the stick as LUMBER (which see) rather than for play. Schultz refers to "dirty woodchoppers like Schmautz and others who gave the league a bad image." (p. 132)

to pull a **zamboni** – to sprawl awkwardly, scraping up snow off the ice. The term comes from the name of the inventor of the machine that cleans and smoothens the ice during breaks between periods, Frank J. Zamboni, the owner of a rink in Paramount, California, in 1949. "He's a regular Zamboni" means "he can't skate very well, he sprawls a lot."

11.

TECHNICAL TERMS, WITH A DIFFERENCE

close to the vest – said of the refereeing in a very tight game in which the referees are watching closely and calling some questionable penalties, to try to keep tempers and violence down.

crowding the crease – said when players congregate in front of the net, giving the goalie increased protection if they are his teammates, and terror if they are not. from Ian Ferguson.

dance – fight. "Once in a while we have a dance, even with a black eye." – *Orr on Ice*, p. 150. "It takes two to tango." – Schultz, p. 1943. Also called "the waltz."

drag – "slowing down from a swift dash over the ice. To do so, one skate blade is 'dragged' in a flat position." – Howard Liss, *Hockey Talk for Beginners.*

drop passes – "where one player would whip across a teammate's path and leave him the puck." – Peter Gzowski, *The Game of Our Lives*, Toronto: McClelland and Steward, 1983, p. 90.

dropping the gloves – customary way to announce during a hockey game that a fight is about to begin. Contrasts with "putting on the gloves," the familiar metaphorical expression in general usage for the same thing.

dump and chase – an offensive strategy in which the puck is shot ahead into the area behind the net and in the corners and the players have to scrap for it. Most students of the game agree that this style of play has come to be used more in the last thirty or forty years. Several explanations of its origins and effects exist. Ken Dryden *(The Game,* p. 217) describes it as a simplified tactic adopted during the years of World War II, when the quality of hockey players was affected by the war, and "less skilled passers, unable to penetrate a packed defense, made no pretense of passing, instead shooting the puck ahead of them to the corners, and chasing after it." Another explanation has it that the size of rinks was reduced as the game became more popular, the ice space confined by the need to fit in seats, so that three defencemen could block off the whole zone: "You can't skate." Almost all agree that the style is less skilled than others. Toe Blake is said to have fined players for playing "dump and chase." See also **shoot and run.**

flood the ice – the term for the procedure by which an outdoor ice rink is tended, the ice made smooth after it is scratched up by the skates. An indoor rink is CLEANED, usually with a **Zamboni,** which see.

freezing the puck – "keeping the puck jammed against the boards with a stick or skates," for a whistle (stop in play). – *Orr on Ice,* p. 164.

game – a contest between two teams, even in French. Also known as **un match, joute.** The word is also encountered as a verb in general Québécois colloquial usage, having spread from its use in hockey: to **gamer** (to vie for, to contest) – as in "il a gamer deux bourses," or "j'ai gamer un nouvelle job."

hits – bodychecks ("Gee, I don't know how many hits there've been tonight, quite a few, though").

legs – a player's speed and skill. "His legs are gone." A player recovering from a slump may be said to have "found his legs."

put a lid on – said of a referee or player who stops something. Sandy Jenkins remembers the old days when "the stem gaze of Bill Friday put a lid on each team's single 'policeman' so that the boys 'kept to hockey.'" – Yellow Sunday, p. 6.

lie – "the angle made by the shaft of the stick and the blade." – Howard Liss, *Hockey Talk for Beginners*.

the long side – see **the short side.**

loose – as in baseball, this word is not always derogatory, but in most contexts, when applied to a team's state of mind before a game, denotes "not uptight or nervous," relaxed, confident.

make a box – to play defensively by assigning players to guard an area of the team's end of the ice, rather than a specific opponent. Used for penalty-killing. from Ian Ferguson.

matchs nuls(Fr) – "tie games."

match-suicide(Fr) – "sudden death game," a game ended in an overtime period in which the first team to score wins, immediately ending play before the expiration of the scheduled, allotted time for the overtime period.

mucking – scrapping for the puck in the corners. DIGGING (which see). Tim Burke of the Montreal *Gazette*, in a column titled "Key for Canada has been Tonelli," writes that Tonelli's career suddenly took off when Bill Dineen of Houston switched him from centre to left wing "on a 'mucking'line."

neutral zone – center ice between the blue lines.

no smoking section – see entry under "Wrong Moves."

pad-save – stopping a shot with the pad.

paper – contract for professional hockey. "He's only good on paper."

paraphernalia – word used by Danny Gallivan to avoid saying "scrotum," "nuts," etc. "He took that shot right between the legs, and as you can see, he's all tangled up in his paraphernalia."

pick-play – an offensive plan whereby the defenceman is forced to choose one of two possible puckcarriers and is manoeuvred into committing himself, at which point the puck is passed to the other. From Bob Beale.

power play – "The team with a man advantage during a penalty sends five men into the short-handed team's defensive zone." Orr, p. 164. The Montreal Canadiens' success with power-play goals led in 1956 to "an important rule change, ending a minor penalty as soon as the power play was scored." – Tim Considine, *The Language of Sport*.

he was on the pro course – he was on his way to the NHL, playing extremely well in municipal league etc. – from Peter and Patty Huse, said of both Peter's cousin and Patty's nephew at age 11 or 12, the memory stirred by watching "The Scarborough ... " second installment of Home Game, CBC-TV, February 11, 1990, which shows how many young players seem to be "on the pro course" who end up not making it. The phrase is perhaps adapted from golf.

pull the goalie – conventional maneuvre by a team which is down during the last minute of a game, in which it takes the goalie off the ice, adding a player to make a last-ditch offensive drive, taking the chance that the other team will get the puck and add to its lead by shooting into the undefended goal. Jonathan Weissman has pointed out that this maneuver is never done by the Russians.

raggedy hockey – hockey in which nothing much is happening. See also RAGGING THE PUCK.

scrum – "the result of a goalie robbing the opposing team of a goal, caused by players on both teams speeding towards the net and stopping abruptly at close quarters. Like 'the gathering of the clan' except that someone from the blue line jumps into the scrum, usually to protect the goalie. Frequently used by Dick Irvin." – from Jonathan Weissman

shoot and run – see **dump and chase.** Dave Schultz says "It is a fact of life that in the contemporary game every team employs the shoot-and-run technique, although it has such obvious flaws ... Doug Harvey ... analyzed (it) with rare disgust. 'I consider it one of the most stupid moves imaginable. When a player voluntarily gives up the puck at center ice and shoots it into the corner, he is, literally, giving the puck away to the other team.'" (p. 204).

shootout – high-scoring, all-out hockey game characterized by end to end play and poor defense. The 1984-85 Edmonton Oilers played and won many games of this sort.

triangle or triangle formation – a way of positioning the three men remaining on the ice when two are in the penalty box at once, a penalty-killing formation. See also **box.**

two on one – short way to describe when two forwards rush against one defenseman, or, less frequent, when two defensemen harry the one puck-carrier. A term also used in basketball.

two up – see **up.**

up – when an announcer says a team is "one up" or "two up," the reference is usually to the number of players on the ice, not to the score. That is, when a team is still at full strength but the opposing team has one or two players off in the penalty box, the first team is one or two men up, has the "man advantage," and is in the "power play" situation. The other team must play a strategy known as "penalty-killing," using the suspension of the normal rule against "icing" to keep shooting the puck down the ice away from its own goal. If the team with fewer members manages to score a goal, it is a "short-handed goal."

up on the roof – a shot into the top part of the goal. See **top drawer.**

on waivers – primarily a description of the contractual process by which a player is let go, this term gets a metaphorical extension in Nancy Dowd's script for the film Slap Shot when one player says to another, both looking at another player's wife who they've heard is estranged from her husband and therefore available, "I hear she's on waivers."

it's tough to go to the wall so many times in a row – to be hard-pressed, behind in the score, meeting a particularly tough team over and over again or a particularly tough defenseman or offense.

the Wave – fan participation hockey ritual in which, starting at rinkside, fans stand up one at a time, from the bottom of the stands to the top, in a line; then the next row does the same, then the next, creating a spectacular WAVE effect. "Now a part of the spectacle of baseball, football, hockey. Originated (according to whom one believes) at Northwestern U. (football) or, predictably, a California University-" – James Herlan, correspondence.

Doug Beardsley claims that it is "a desperate attempt by the [Vancouver] fans to show that they are still there, that they still matter in arenas that are increasingly designed as 'multi-purpose facilities' rather than hockey rinks." ... "The first impression of the Pacific Coliseum is of smallness. It's as if the upper level of the arena has been cut off, leaving only the 'reds' and 'blues' seating... how far we are from the ice; the seats slant upward at less of an angle than at the Gardens in Toronto or the Forum in Montreal... The fan is further away from the action than in most NHL arenas. As a result, I find that one has the feeling of being dissociated from the play... " - *Country on Ice*, p. 84-85.

wing the puck – to shoot the puck to the left or right side corner behind the goal.

woodwork – used on the CBC October 28, 1985, to describe a crosscheck in which Stasny hit an opponent high with the stick.

work – see **finesse players.** In most uses this word means more to do with **mucking** (which also see) than with goal-scoring play. It also carries the connotation of violent, aggressive style and tactics.

wrist shot – a snap or flick, rather than a slapshot or two-hander.

wrong wing – left winger skating on the right side, or a right winger on the left.

playing the **zone** – a defensive strategy for penaltykilling, when the defense has fewer players on the ice than the offense. It consists in assigning players an area to defend, instead of a particular opponent, one on one. See also **make a box.** – from Ian Ferguson.

12. Hockey talking:
WORDS ABOUT TALK

Bas – On the **Hot Stove League** on CBC radio Saturday night Canadiens' broadcast, between periods, Basil O'Meara was "the long-winded, tiresome repeater of clichés, all season long. By playoff time the sound of his voice would irritate so much, you'd be leaving to pee, raid ice box, etc., whenever the chairman asked 'How did you see the first period, Bas?' Thus **Bas** became a term for 'a long-winded bore' and by extension to the rink or street, someone who hogged the puck and never scored." See also **Elmer.**

chirping – "mouthing off," especially when done by a fan in the stands who is heckling a player on the ice, according to George Plimpton, *Open Net*, New York: W W Norton, 1985, p. 28.

and the deuces are wild! – Dick Irvin's classic obsen‚ation when the score is tied 2-2 in the 2nd period, or there is 2:22 remaining in a period, especially the 2nd. – from Jonathan Weissman.

Elmer – On the **Hot Stove League** (which see), on CBC radio Canadiens broadcast between periods, Elmer " spoke little compared to Bas (see **Bas)** and what he said never seemed to have much to do with the topic at hand, or beside the point, etc. Thus, an ELMER, the useless, irrelevant, etc. On the rink or street, the Icind of guy who gave the puck away, or passed to the wrong man, scored on his own team, etc."

exchanging pleasantries – announcer's understatement to describe two players commencing a fight.

Hockey Reading and Sources List

Aléong, Stanley. "L'histoire du vocabulaire quebecois du hockey sur glace." La *Banque des Mots*, 20: 1980. Pp. 195-210.

Aléong, Stanley. "Usage populaire et dirigisme linguistique dans le vocabulaire québécois du hockey sur glace." in Klinkenberg, Jean-Marie, Danielle Racelle-Latin, et Guy Cannally, eds. *Langages et Collectives: le cas du Qu6b6c*. Actes du Colloque du Liège 1980. Montreal: Leméac, 1981. Pp. 133-144.

Beardsley, Doug. *Country on* Ice. Toronto: Paperjacks, 1988.

Beddoes, Fischler, Gitler, *Hockey! The Story of the World's Fastest Sport*. New York: Macmillan, 1971.

Blanchard, Kendall, and Alyce Cheska, *The Anthropology of Sport*. Boston: Bergin and Garvey, 1985.

Bowering, George (ed.) *Great Canadian Sports Stories*. Oberon, 1979. See especially "The Drubbing of Nesterenko," by Hanford Woods.

BVB Research. *Pocket Hockey Encyclopedia*. Toronto: Pagurian Press, 1972.

Carrier, Roch. *The Hockey Sweater and other Stories*. Translated by Sheila Fischman. Toronto: Anansi, 1979. Originally published as *Les Enfants du bonhomme dans la lune*. Montreal: Stanké, 1979.

Considine, Tim. *The Language of Sport*. New York: World Almanac, 1982.

Dallaire, Pierre. *Lexique de termes de hockey francais-anglais.* Montréal: Lemeac, 1983.

*Dictionary of Canadianisms on Historical Principles.*ed. Walter Avis. Toronto, 1967.

Dryden, Ken. *The Game.* Toronto: Macmillan of Canada,1983.

Eskenazi, Gerald. A *Thinking Man's Guide to Hockey,* rev. ed. Dutton, New York, 1976.

Farrington, S. Kip. Jr. *Skates, Sticks and Men: The Story of Amateur Hockey in the United States.* New York:David McKay Co., Inc., 1972.

Fischler, Stan. Amazing *Trivia from the World of Hockey,* New York: Penguin, 1983.

Fischler, Stan. *Bobby Orr and the Big, Bad Bruins.* New York: Dell. 1969.

Fischler, Stan and Shirley Walton Fischler. *The Hockey Encyclopedia.* New York: MacMillan, 1983.

Fitsell, J.W. *Hockey's Captains, Colonels & Kings.* Erin, Ont. Boston Mills Press, 1987.

Goyens, Chrys and Allan Turowetz. Lions *in Winter.* Scarborough, Ont.: Prentice-Hall, 1986.

Green, Ted and AI Hirshberg. *High Stick.* New York: Dodd, Mead, & Co., 1971.

Gzowski, Peter. *The Game of Our Lives.* Rev. ed. Toronto: Macmillan of Canada, 1982.

Herlan, James J. ,The Montreal Canadiens: A Hockey Metaphor," *Quebec Studies*, 1:1 (Spring 1983), pp. 96-108.

Herlan, James J. "Buffalo's Icy Love Affair," *Buffalo Spree*, 19:1 (Spring 1985), pp. 88-92.

Hood, Hugh. *Strength Down Centre: The Jean Beliveau Story*. Scarborough: Prentice-Hall of Canada, 1970.

Irvin, Dick. *Now Back to You Dick: Two Lifetimes in Hockey*. Toronto: McClelland and Stewart, 1989.

Jenkins, Sandy. *Yellow Sunday: Making and breaking the rules in the LNH*. Beauceville, Quebec: JenkinsSpeak, 1988.

Jeremiah, Eddie. *Ice Hockey*. New York: Barnes and Noble. 1942.

Kelly, Sean. "The Canadiens and Soul Hockey," *New York Times* (Sunday, April 9, 1978), See. 5, p. 2.

Kinoy, Ernest. *The Deadliest Season. 1982*.

Liss, Howard. *Hockey Talk for Beginners*. New York: Julian Messner, 1973.

MacGregor, Roy. *The Last Season*. Toronto: Macmillan of Canada, 1983.

MacLennan, Hugh. "Fury on Ice," in *The Other Side of Hugh MacLennan*, ed. Elspeth Cameron. Toronto: Macmillan of Canada, 1978, pp. 69-82.

McFarlane, Brian. *50 Years of Hockey*. Toronto: Pagurian Press, n.d.

McIlhone, Quinn. *Trade Rumors*. Toronto: McClelland and Stewart, 1985.

Murdoch, Don. *Thin Ice* (New York Post excerpts from the 1970).

O'Brien, Andy. *Superstars: Hockey's Greatest Players*. Toronto: McGraw-Hill Ryerson, 1973.

Orr, Bobby with Dick Grace. *Orr On Ice*. New York: Prentice-Hall, 1970.

Pagnucco, Frank. *Heroes: Stars of Hockey's Golden Era*. New York: Prentice-Hall, 1985.

Plimpton, George. *Open Net*. New York: WW Norton, 1985.

Richler, Mordecai. *Home Sweet Home: My Canadian Album*. New York: Alfred A. Knopf. 1984.

Schultz, Dave, with Stan Fischler. *The Hammer: Confessions of a Hockey Enforcer*. Toronto: Totem Books,1982.

Scriver, Stephen. *The All-Star Poet*. Moose Jaw, Sask.: Thunder Creek Publishing Cooperative, 1981.

"The Sporting Scene: Les Canadiens Sont Là," *The New Yorker*, March 19, 1979, pp. 80-125.

Stokes, Lynette, ed., with Fawn Duchaine. *Unsportsmanlike Conduct*, Montreal: Eden Press, 1985.

Thain, Chris. *Cold as a Bay Street Banker's Heart: The Ultimate Prairie Phrase Book*. 1989.

Thom, Douglas J. *The Hockey Bibliography: Ice Hockey Worldwide.* Ontario Institute for Studies in Education, 1978.

Young, Scott. *Scrubs on Skates.* Toronto: McClelland and Stewart, 1952, 1985.

INDEX

117